Shaping Your Future Leadership

Shaping Your Future Leadership

Learning From Your Life Experiences

Peter Shaw

CANTERBURY
PRESS
Norwich

© Peter Shaw 2023

Published in 2023 by Canterbury Press
Editorial office
3rd Floor, Invicta House,
108–114 Golden Lane,
London EC1Y 0TG, UK
www.canterburypress.co.uk

Canterbury Press is an imprint of Hymns Ancient & Modern Ltd
(a registered charity)

Hymns Ancient & Modern® is a registered trademark of
Hymns Ancient & Modern Ltd
13A Hellesdon Park Road, Norwich,
Norfolk NR6 5DR, UK

British Library Cataloguing in Publication data

A catalogue record for this book is available
from the British Library

Scripture quotations marked (NIV) are taken from
The Holy Bible, New International Version (Anglicised edition)
copyright © 1979, 1984, 2011 by Biblica (formerly International
Bible Society). Used by permission of Hodder & Stoughton Publishers,
an Hachette UK company. All rights reserved.

978-1-78622-523-8

Typeset by Regent Typesetting
Printed and bound in Great Britain by
CPI Group (UK) Ltd

'Be kind, be brave, be true' are the words emblazed on the t-shirt of my grandson Stellan who was born on the same day as me, albeit 71 years later. I dedicate this book to all those with leadership responsibilities who are seeking to be kind, brave and true.

Contents

G Look Ahead With Grounded Hope 95

Foreword

I was disappointed on being given my first formal leadership role – in the National Health Service in the early 1990s – to find that my new job title did not confer any superpowers. I was still the same old me! Confident sometimes, at other times plagued with imposter syndrome. Able to connect with some people and destined to have friction with others. Sometimes kind, encouraging and inspiring, sometimes stressed, tetchy and sarcastic. My intellectual and emotional intelligence seemed to come and go – sometimes the two worked together, other times my head and my heart seemed hell-bent on fighting each other to the death.

I obviously did OK despite this, because I did go on to have a successful career in leadership. Having Peter Shaw as my coach for five years in the noughties was part of that process – it allowed me to accept that it was OK to be an ordinary person who happens to be a leader. Over the years I have come to believe, as Peter does, that great leaders are created from ordinary people who are prepared to understand their own strengths and weaknesses, who will invest in getting to know and understand others, who will seek and listen to feedback and who will, most importantly, carry on being open and curious. Such an ordinary person with these qualities will be a much more effective leader than an exceptional person without them.

I am mentioned in this book – I was one of the six people the UK Cabinet Office asked Peter to see when he was beginning his second career as a coach in 2004. We had an immediate connection (despite my occasional bouts of tetchy sarcasm) and he became my coach for five years and a lifelong touchstone. We have continued to meet regularly and I am always inspired by his simple, practical take on leadership, based on his instincts, his own experience and 20 years of coaching hundreds of top leaders.

Since my first meeting with Peter, I am pleased to see that many aspects of his philosophy have become the norm in leadership. Back in 2004, when I was a Director in the UK Civil Service, a certain façade was expected. Leaders were expected to behave in ways that emphasized formality, authority, self-assurance – qualities that were signalled by the word 'impact', and which were trained into leaders through modelling and sometimes formal courses. Relationships were kept 'professional' – sharing personal information was kept to a minimum, and most especially any imprudent or shaming experiences were kept well hidden. Since those days, organizations have learned that building inclusive, diverse teams where people feel able to be their full selves leads to better outcomes. This has changed the requirements of leaders in ways we could not have imagined in 2004. The generations that succeeded mine – the Millennials and Gen Z – expect leaders who will connect with them, humanize the workplace and accept diversity even when it is uncomfortable. They will not tolerate overbearing, egotistical behaviour, dismissive or disrespectful language, undermining micro-behaviours or any of the other subtle aggressions which used to make some workplace politics so miserable. They want to know their leaders and they expect us to be authentic, approachable and human.

In demanding this higher level of humanity, the new generations have made the workplace better for everyone. They have set a high bar for leaders, who now have to demonstrate stronger emotional literacy than ever before. The need to cultivate this emotional literacy in order to become a great leader is a theme that has featured in all of Peter's books, but this book is his most personal take to date. Part memoir, part guidebook, Peter takes us on a journey from understanding our very earliest experiences to making sure we have the right balance and options into older years. Nobody can ever expect to be a perfect leader (or a perfect anything for that matter) but becoming the best leader you can be is an inspiring proposition, and Peter is a compassionate, questioning and rewarding companion on that journey.

Julie Taylor
Chief Financial Officer for National Grid Ventures
London, UK

Introduction

The fast pace of change requires us to be deliberate in shaping our future leadership. We cannot stand by and just be observers. Our responsibility as leaders is to help shape the future and not let ourselves be overwhelmed by it. To do that well we need a combination of courage and contemplation, pace and patience, alongside hope and humility.

Leaders who are reasonably comfortable in themselves recognize what shapes them. They bring an understanding and interpretation of their past and what family, cultural, educational and faith contexts have formed them. They continually learn from their life journey and that of others. They are fully engaged in the present, and have a positive, open and realistic mindset in approaching the future.

This book will provide prompts to help you develop a deeper understanding of what has shaped you as a leader and how best you can develop your qualities in the next phase of your leadership.

The intended outcomes are to enable leaders to:

- Be more comfortable in themselves as they better understand their history and experiences
- Recognize how best to draw from their own past in moving deliberately into their future
- Recognize how future responsibilities will continue to shape them and others
- Be better equipped to live with their emotions and know what energizes them going forward, and
- Bring a positive view to the future, whatever uncertainties they are currently going through.

I have had the privilege of working at senior levels in the public sector for over 30 years and for 20 years in the private sector. It has been a joy to work with leaders and teams on six continents from many different backgrounds and with very different world views. Various people suggested that I distil what I have observed into this book and use stories from my own personal experience to bring to life the themes that seem most pertinent for individuals looking to shape their future leadership. I am so grateful to those companions on the way who have helped build resilience and resolve in me. Their encouragement and support have been crucial.

The intent is to provide illustrations and prompts that are relevant for individuals at any stage of their working lives as they think about moving into different and potentially more senior roles or into leadership roles in the voluntary sector with a portfolio of different types of responsibility. I hope the themes work just as well for the 25-year-old and the 75-year-old.

The heart of my approach to enabling leaders to step up is seeking to inspire them to apply the Four Vs of Leadership: to develop their personal *vision* of the leader they are seeking to be; to be cognizant of the *values* that they are seeking to live by; to be deliberate in the *value-add* they want to bring to the next phase of their leadership; and to recognize how best to sustain their *vitality*.

This book sets out seven lenses through which to reflect on your beliefs and mindset as a leader, namely:

A Understand the legacy from your formative years
B Own your life decisions
C Recognize your voice and influence
D Recognize the shadow you cast
E Live with your emotions
F Know what energizes
G Look ahead with grounded hope

I devote a section to each lens: each section explores five areas and concludes with some questions for reflection. In the concluding chapter, I seek to bring the themes together and invite the reader to think through:

- The alignment between different interests, preferences and priorities
- Your acceptance of who you are and the types of opportunities available to you
- The sense of adventure that can shape your mindset and choices.

I hope that the approach in the book is helpful for you. It draws on the approach in the book *Creativity Inc* written by Ed Catmull which combines key lessons about leadership with stories from his professional life as a leader in the animation industry.

Recent world events have forced us to recognize both the uncertainties we face and the needs and opportunities we can address. Hence the value of reflecting on our individual leadership journeys and how we can best take the initiative in choosing what leadership contribution we want to make in the next phase of our life journey.

Peter Shaw
Surrey, England

A

Understand the Legacy from Your Formative Years

We are all shaped by the first 20 years of life but do not always recognize the full significance of the experiences in those formative years. In coaching conversations, I will often begin with an exploration of key influences in the formative years and how an individual has been shaped through parental, community, educational and societal influences.

Being able to observe those influences and not just be captive to them can be liberating. Homing in on the distinctive qualities that come from your upbringing and heritage provides a framework that can give credence to your strengths and explanations for your foibles.

1 Parents and wider family

Our childhood years will have had a bigger influence on us than we perhaps care to admit. We have been shaped by our interactions with parents and grandparents and other family members. The type of care and development we receive from close family members will have had a profound influence on our hopes and fears. Our parents will not always have made the best decisions. Sometimes there will be deeply rooted anxieties that have resulted from the beliefs or actions of our parents.

I owe a great deal to the commitment of my mother to bringing up a very unconfident child following my father's death when I was seven. My mother was the youngest of six children, who trained in domestic science and ran the works canteen at the ICI Dyestuffs factory in Huddersfield. When many of the male workers joined the forces in 1940, she took on a role recruiting and looking after the welfare of women doing jobs that had previously been done by men. She was the first female member of the management team at ICI in Huddersfield and the first woman to be allowed to drive a car into the office carpark.

When my mother got married in 1945, she had to resign from work because of the expected norms at the time about male precedence. My mother was shaped by her Methodist background and her commitment to her family. There was a quiet confidence and faith which enabled her to maintain a steadiness and cheerfulness through 40-plus years as a widow.

My father worked in an accountancy practice, supporting the qualified partners. He was always regarded as thorough and reliable. He was a steward at the local Methodist church. After his first heart attack in 1956, a TV was bought which enabled him to watch Jim Laker take 19 wickets in one cricket Test match against Australia that summer. Sadly, he died later that year.

I never knew any grandparents but have always been struck by the story of my mother's father who began work as an office boy at a woollen mill at Huddersfield and studied French at an evening class. When a letter came into the mill written in French, a request went out within the mill for anyone who could read French. My grandfather volunteered: the management were impressed by his learning and enterprise and began to give him additional responsibilities, eventually leading to his becoming the mill manager. My grandfather was an illustration to me of being willing to keep learning and then take opportunities.

As my mother's primary income was the state widow's pension, finances were tight throughout my childhood. Clothes were worn until they were worn out. Food was never wasted; we ate the cheaper cuts of meat. My mother was an excellent cook and produced a wide range of different cakes and buns which would not have been consistent with current beliefs about minimizing sugar intake! One aunt had taught in primary education throughout a fulfilling career and developed in me a delight in the use of English. The book *First Aid in English* became a regular source of shared enjoyment.

I am conscious that my parents, and especially my mother, shaped my approach to life. They brought a combination of calmness and resolve. They had come through the war years and were not going to be beaten down by sadness or disappointment. The only time I remember my father getting cross was when I had punched holes in a hot water bottle full of water using a small screwdriver. When he picked up the hot water bottle and carried it downstairs, he felt a dampness as the water from the water bottle leaked onto his trousers.

I grew up in the small town of Bridlington on the East Yorkshire coast. My mother recognized that there was little likelihood that I would stay in the town when I left school. Her calmness when I went to Durham University and then studied in Vancouver before moving to London was impressive. I took that calm acceptance for granted in my youth, but now recognize that, as a single parent, she was giving space for her only child to find his own way in life. It was far tougher for my mother as a single parent with an only child than it was for Frances and me when our three children left home to go to university.

My mother delighted in attending two of my graduation ceremonies, in Durham and Bradford, but sadly died a couple of years before I received an honour from the Queen. (The honour has the antiquated title of CB, Companion of the Order of the Bath.) Attending that ceremony would have been a very special fulfilment for her. There is a bench dedicated to her at Winkworth Arboretum in Surrey with views over glades of trees that are full of colour in the autumn. We periodically go and sit on her bench and eat crunch or gingerbread made according to her family recipes.

The overriding values I draw from my family background are steadiness, calmness and faithfulness with a deliberate carefulness about finance and a cautiousness about risk.

Reflections

1. How have your parents shaped your way of thinking and your emotional reactions?
2. Who are your role models from your wider family who have shaped your aspirations?
3. What are aspects of, or moments from, your family background that may act as inhibitors where you need to be bolder?

2 Community

When coaching an individual, I will often try to gain an understanding of their family background and the community context in which they grew up. Having an insight into their community context is invaluable in understanding the perspective that they are likely to bring to different situations.

As an example, I am struck by the number of people I engage with holding senior posts in prisons who have come from a Roman Catholic background. My observation is that often people from a Catholic background combine a deep care for people alongside a recognition of the fallibility of human nature. This type of compassion for people living with the results of their own frailties, combined with a belief that people can change if the structures are right, has helped mould the attitude of a good number of leaders in prison administration.

Those people who have been involved in community activities in their youth often make good team members, able to draw out the strengths and compensate for the foibles of others. For some there is the recognition that the aggression of their youth has toned down over the years. The legacy of this is often a willingness to show determination but with a greater modulation about how it is expressed.

I was brought up in a small Yorkshire town with a population that was much bigger in the summer. There were streets of boarding houses where people from the West Riding of Yorkshire came to stay to spend time on the Bridlington beaches in the 1950s. The amusement arcades were definitely for the tourists and not the impressionable younger residents of the town: I remember being seriously reprimanded by my mother on one occasion when I wandered into an amusement arcade. Many years later when we had children, we would sometimes visit a tenpin bowling alley in Bridlington that was in the midst of an amusement arcade. When we went with my mother, she averted her eyes and focused straight ahead as we walked through these banks of 'gambling' machines.

The community in which I grew up in the 1950s was disciplined, polite and still recovering from the war years. We crowded around a neighbour's small TV set to watch the coronation in 1953, but normally socializing was done on the street and not in the house. Occasionally there would be tea on the beach with a particular teapot and the chipped cups reserved for this purpose carried down to the beach on an ancient rusty metal tray. When a neighbour bought their first car there was the excitement of a new vehicle with indicators that flashed rather than little arms on the side of the car which popped up when the driver wished to turn off the road.

The community became noisier in the '60s with the advent of pop concerts at the Spa Royal Hall. A succession of '60s pop bands meant that Bridlington was on the pop scene and being a teenager in this Yorkshire town did not feel as isolated. The Searchers, Freddie and the Dreamers and Gerry and the Pacemakers all delighted the youth of East Yorkshire, including me.

People in the town and district worked on the industrial estate, in tourism, agriculture and local town public and private services. The community was white and conservative. Day trippers were to be tolerated because they brought money into the town.

Tourism provided me with my first work experiences. My first job was washing up at a local restaurant where an octogenarian had very strict rules about how utensils were to be washed and dried. My second job was selling ice creams on Bridlington pier where favoured customers got ice cream inside the cone as well as on top of the cone. Later I drove a delivery van for a butcher in the morning and stacked shelves for a grocer in the afternoon. Both these experiences taught me about finding your place in a small team and building relationships with people whose horizons were locally focused but who brought special human qualities of kindness and reliability.

The Methodist church was central to my experience of community. It brought together people of different ages and from different walks of life. There was a shared sense of engagement and purpose among people whose financial and personal circumstances were very different. What rubbed off on me was the importance of having a shared purpose alongside an acceptance that people's levels of commitment and interest will vary in terms of how they want to contribute outside their immediate family. I particularly remember some small acts of generosity which had a lasting effect on me.

I am conscious that the people I work with who come from a Hindu, Sikh, Moslem, Buddhist or Jewish background talk equally passionately about the influence of the faith communities they grew up in as exemplars of encouraging and supportive communities.

My childhood home was within 100 yards of the sea promenade in Bridlington. The sound and smell of the sea was always there in the background. Walking on the cliffs from Bridlington to Sewerby, and then on to Flamborough, was a delight. Our dining room walls include various water colour paintings of the chalk cliffs between Bridlington and Flamborough. There is the strength and relentlessness about the waves beating onto the beach in a storm, or quietly flowing up the beach on a calm day.

Living by the sea gave me an appreciation of the rhythms of the seasons and the need to respect the forces of the natural environment. Whatever castles in the sand were built, they rarely survived the beatings from the waves. Yet there was a temporary satisfaction of building sand barriers that held back the encroaching sea, at least for a little while. My parents are buried in Bridlington so we try to combine a visit each year to the cemetery with walks along the chalk cliffs at Flamborough, Sewerby and Bempton. The fresh sea air is always bracing and uplifting.

Reflections

1. What are the lasting influences from the communities you were part of as a child?
2. What aspect of the community norms did you not feel comfortable with, or began to rebel against, in your youth and how has that shaped your current thinking?
3. What underlying values do you seek to build in any community you are part of which have their roots in your formative years?

3 Education

The type of education we experienced inevitably has a huge effect on how we view the world. Where education has been enjoyable, it has developed curiosity and a sense of exploration and excitement about learning. Where education has been painful, it may have left a wariness about being in enclosed learning situations with others and a fear of being caught out.

In our first years at school, were we able to be part of the group or did we become isolated and hesitant? There was the forbidding prospect of the exam at age 11 which would determine whether you went to a grammar school or a secondary modern school for the secondary phase of education. The 11+ exam gave many in my generation either a drive to succeed or a sense of being a failure.

Education has opened up the horizon for so many people, allowing the opportunity to engage with different philosophies and cultures. The lasting influence of key teachers is often one of the most powerful experiences that has shaped leaders' attitudes to learning.

My main memory of the nursery school I attended was the periodic award of a token for a free ice cream for good behaviour. The prospect of an ice cream was a remarkably powerful incentive. My primary school years were overshadowed by the death of my father in my first year at primary school. I became withdrawn and unwilling to contribute. The kindly encouragement of John Taylor, my form teacher in the third year, helped me become more confident: I began to enjoy the country dancing, although my partner always accused me of 'having two left feet.'

I came into my own in my early years in secondary school where the grammar school environment suited my quiet, studious personality. I was less diligent at the peak of my teenage years but was fortunate enough to be in an outstanding class where virtually everyone received ten ordinary level passes at age 16. A very influential teacher was John Lepper (Sid as he was nicknamed because of his Birmingham accent). I still correspond with John who is now over 90. John brought a wonderful sense of humour as a means of encouraging pupils to give of their best.

The sixth form years reinforced my love of geography with a growing delight in hill walking. An outstanding teacher, David Rhodes, stretched my thinking and encouraged me to think about going to Cambridge University, which felt a step too far. I felt intimidated by those with posh accents and did not see myself holding my own with people from very different backgrounds to mine.

Perhaps the biggest influence from school was becoming captain of the school second cricket eleven. We had an outstanding season which helped build my confidence in deploying a good range of bowlers. Receiving half colours for cricket at school gave me an enormous sense of satisfaction. I learnt the importance of building a relationship with each member of the team and recognizing what type of encouragement worked best for each player. It taught me to be deliberate in the tactics and philosophic about how a game would play out. For the first time I was seeing how I could be a leader and that others might even follow what I suggested.

As a cricket team we played two extra-curricular games. One was against a girls' school where we were roundly told off for not taking the match seriously enough. I arranged a fixture against a local village side where the pitch was surrounded by big, dark trees. We bowled the village side out for 20 and thought we would romp home to victory. We were then skittled out for 13 runs as two strong local farm workers demolished our batting. Leading our cricket team through the delights of victory alongside the humiliation of defeat was valuable learning.

Going to Durham University widened my horizons far beyond the small-town community of Bridlington. I engaged and became friends with people from quite different social and educational settings. Those I blended with most were, like me, studious products of grammar schools. I enjoyed walking in the Durham Dales, playing cricket for Bede College, being on the executive for the Christian Union, being introduced to Anglican liturgy, delighting in Gilbert and Sullivan concerts, and developing a fascination for Sunderland Football Club. I had my first serious girlfriend at Durham who humanized me. I learnt a lot about the ingredients of good companionship.

As I look back, I think that I began to be my own person when I was 16. At that point I began to make my own life decisions beyond the confines of my sheltered background. Durham University was where I grew up and began to stretch my thinking and become more aware of my own emotions. There was the delight of receiving a respectable degree in 1970. At that point I would never have dreamt that I would receive an honorary doctorate from Durham University 45 years later.

Reflections

1. Which teachers have had a lasting effect on you that you cherish?
2. At what stages in your education and teenage experiences did you grow significantly as an individual?
3. Where have you had to break out from some of the inhibiting factors that have resulted from your educational experiences?

4 Societal context

The societal context of the first 20 years of our lives feed into the way we think. Just as a mother's milk influences the development of the baby, so the ambience of the society in which we spent our first 20 years has shaped us. For those of us whose formative years were in the '50s and '60s, the post-war period was a time of rationing and shortages followed by being told by the Prime Minister of the day that, 'we had never had it so good.'

The '60s saw societal norms radically changing. There were bitter struggles with the unions that affected many households in the '70s and into the '80s. The Cold War of the '60s into the '80s created a heaviness, alleviated by the exciting stories of expeditions to the moon. The '90s seemed to bring a new world order with the end of the Soviet Union and apartheid in South Africa. Middle Eastern wars and religious terrorism brought a new heaviness, heightened by the events of 9/11 in 2001. The Covid pandemic of 2020–2022, the increasingly obvious effects of climate change, and the invasion of Ukraine have brought a new level of cautiousness and unease.

The most radical societal changes over our lifetimes have resulted from changes in technology, with profound consequences for the ways in which we communicate with one another. Letter writing and occasional phone calls have been replaced by a myriad of immediate communication. Emotional reactions are instantly transmitted with limited thought for how they are going to be received. Communications have become increasingly blunt, one-dimensional and unforgiving, often avoiding the underlying issues of greatest concern.

Each of us is strongly influenced by the societal context of the current era. But we were also shaped by the societal context of the first 20 years of our lives, as it shaped the parenting we received and the information we were fed through the communications of that era.

My mother had made a major contribution to the war effort through her work at ICI, enabling women to do jobs previously done by men. She had been part of a breakthrough whereby the contribution of women doing influential jobs was increasingly recognized. Yet when she moved to Bridlington and a few years later was widowed, the expectation was that she stay at home and bring up an unconfident child. The societal expectations were that it would not be appropriate for her to go out to work: her role was to stay at home and focus on bringing up her son and look after her sister who was in poor health.

The fear of bombing and possible defeat had left people in the UK exhausted at the end of the Second World War: this left a legacy in the UK of a fairly unambitious and benign society. The UK was having to come to terms with a lesser influence in the world order. My father died the year after the Suez humiliation. By the start of the 1960s there was a new optimism. The Prime Minister, Harold Macmillan, talked about 'the winds of change', but they did not become apparent until Harold Wilson began to talk about the 'white heat of technology'. There was a new hopefulness for the future with the Labour Government of 1964 to 1970 following England's success in the football world cup in 1966.

As a teenager I was compliant. I was firmly told that wearing jeans on Christmas day was not appropriate. My most rebellious act was eating large ice creams. I once stood up a girl who I had asked out by turning up at the due time and then saying I was going to play table tennis instead of taking her out to a James Bond film. A few months later I was stood up by a girl who had said yes to going out for a meal. I was learning (or not learning) some social norms.

My level of rebellion in the late '60s was very low. There was a growing sense that those of us fortunate enough to go to university in the '60s, which at that point was a tiny minority, had an obligation to seek to make a difference in the world. We had the benefit of grants which provided a degree of independence from the age of 18.

We observed the robustness of the Soviet response in Czechoslovakia and the brutality of the apartheid regime in South Africa. We were conscious of fighting in Vietnam with little prospect of a peaceful outcome. We were conscious that we were geographically part of Europe but outside the Common Market.

For those of us at university in the late '60s, there was an optimism about our own futures within the UK against a background of a gloomy, political context. We felt that, to an extent, we were a 'chosen people' by virtue of our higher education and had a responsibility to seek to make a constructive difference in the wider world. I had been offered a graduate entry role at Marks & Spencer's but decided to study at Regent College adjacent to the campus of the University of British Columbia in Canada. I was open to a very different adventure.

Reflections

1. What societal pressures from the first 20 years of your life have left the biggest mark upon you?
2. What societal influences were most dominant from your parents?
3. What were the sources of optimism in your youth that flowed from the societal changes around you?

5 Inbuilt expectations

By virtue of our family, cultural and community backgrounds there will be inbuilt expectations about behaviours, attitudes and life decisions. Many of these expectations are helpful in giving us a framework for the way we live our lives. Inevitably, some of these expectations will jar and be incompatible with our personal preferences and our decisions about work, relationships and life priorities. If we ride roughshod over our inbuilt expectations, it can result in conflict, which may find its expression in anxiety, anguish or anger.

Becoming comfortable in ourselves means looking objectively at the expectations placed upon us from our backgrounds and then being as dispassionate as possible in recognizing where and why our expectations differ from those we have inherited.

Sometimes the expectations of our parents and our wider community will have moved on, just as ours have. On other occasions those expectations might have become frozen in time with a growing discrepancy between the expectations placed on us and the expectations we now own and live by.

Expectations might come from norms of courtesy, the nature of marriage, or the degree of respect accorded to people of older generations. There might be strong expectations about the type of work someone does. The coalminer may have expected his son to follow him down the pit. There might have been subliminal pressure on the children of a teacher or doctor to follow their parent into the same profession.

There may still be the pressure on some that the man be the main source of income, with the husband who is committed to spending time with the children on a full-time basis being negatively branded a 'stay-at-home husband'. Thankfully, many of these cultural assumptions about what is gender-appropriate behaviour have been eroded over the years, with a much wider range of successful patterns of working, earning and childcare arrangements in families.

I was conscious that there were expectations on me. Whenever I did well at school my mother would say, 'Your father would have been very proud of you.' I fully understand why my mother used that compliment, but I think it did have the effect of putting pressure on me to meet the expectations of the father who had died a few years earlier. Being the only child from my parents' marriage meant that the family focus was on me to study hard. Thankfully, there was no sense of disapproval if my tests results were not as good as they might have been, but I did notice when affirmation was present and when not. There was an expectation that I would stay on at school to do my advanced level exams and then go to university. I am immensely grateful that this was the expectation.

I was strongly influenced by growing up in the Methodist Church and being part of a Christian boys club and then being a member of the Youth Fellowship at an evangelical free church. This combination developed in me a conviction that I should seek to make a difference for good in whatever work I eventually did. I had a sense that I needed to search out the right vocation or calling for me. It also gave me a fascination with the way Jesus used stories and parables in order to help shape the thinking and desires of those he engaged with. In addition, as the grammar school I attended was all boys, it was at the youth fellowship that I built an understanding of how to relate to girls.

My inbuilt expectations were met with a very different world at university. Alcohol at home was a glass of sherry on Christmas day. The college bar seemed like alien territory, and I only gradually came to appreciate the pub as a social meeting place. The college chapel introduced me to the delight of historic Anglican liturgy: it provided a place of calm in an otherwise hectic environment.

Expectations about studying hard and writing essays on time were not a problem. I was fortunate enough not to feel distracted by the headiness of student life in the late 1960s. Being part of the Christian subculture and having a steady girlfriend who was a vicar's daughter meant that there was little temptation to stray from the expectations I had grown up with.

There was a growing curiosity about governance and politics. Studying geography made me very conscious of how different countries went in different directions. There was also a growing desire to experience life outside the UK and to seek to integrate my understanding of community and society that came from studying geography, alongside a desire to apply the relevance of Christian insights to the governance and well-being of organizations. Studying geography looked as if it would naturally lead to town planning which was heavily in vogue, but that was not to be.

Reflections

1. What expectations do you place on yourself which come from deep within you?
2. When have expectations from others been hard to resist?
3. What expectations from your formative years now seem outdated and irrelevant?

B

Own Your Life Decisions

There are life decisions that work well and other decisions that do not turn out as we had hoped. We can go through life with regrets about life decisions that turned out to be mistakes, or only partially effective, or we can go through life remembering what we learnt from decisions that proved to be suboptimal. If all our life decisions proved to be right, there may be a risk of boredom or self-righteousness. If we have a catalogue of decisions that have all gone wrong, we can feel broken, although out of the mire of despondency there can come a strengthened character and new hope. The reality is that we are living with the results of decisions that have both good sides and bad.

Key to being comfortable in yourself as a leader is owning a narrative about life decisions that celebrates the ones that have worked out well and accepts when decisions have not worked out as well as hoped and the learning that has flowed from those decisions.

6 Education and training

Education and training cannot stop at 16, 18 or 21. Those people who thrive have an insatiable appetite for learning. Being able to follow our curiosity is a special gift that opens up new horizons and keeps us alert to possibilities.

Being realistic about how we learn is key. For some, the best way of learning is through an academic route of study and writing essays. For others, learning is embedded through developing skills and then practising them on a regular basis. We are all learning through a combination of life experiences and shocks.

I encourage leaders to learn through observing others and spending time shadowing people they respect. Observing people in different environments can have a profound impact in terms of appreciating how people in different roles have tackled similar problems.

Being a parent is one sort of 'on the job' training: learning to manage toddler tantrums or teenage churlishness helps develop techniques in bringing the best out of a wide range of different characters.

I am conscious that education does not stop at a particular age. Even in my 60s and 70s, I have continued to draw on different life experiences in my understanding of cultures and contexts. Learning is a never-ending process that is a mix of refining what we are good at and developing new techniques and approaches. The learning from each phase then provides us with a unique perspective to inform the next phase.

Studying geography at Durham University for three years gave me an understanding of the importance of place and the interconnections between different geographic, social and economic considerations. It stimulated me to think through the effects of being caught by the consequences of geography, and when geographic realities present opportunities that should not be wasted.

After graduating from Durham University in 1970, I spent a year doing a Diploma in Christian Studies at Regent College on the campus of the University of British Columbia in Vancouver. The college had been set up with a focus on lay people who would be going into careers in the secular world but wanted to bring an understanding informed by their Christian faith. This was a hugely formative year for me in a different country. I worked as a painter and decorator to earn enough to live on. I was in the first tranche of full-time students at the college and, therefore, we became ambassadors for the college. I subsequently completed a Masters' degree at the college and have taught there regularly as a visiting professor since 2008.

The geography degree should have led naturally into town planning. I was awarded a place at Bradford University to do a Masters' degree in transport engineering and planning. Early on in the course, I concluded that I did not want to pursue a career in transport or planning. The retired Vice Principal at Bede College in Durham suggested that I apply for the graduate intake into the Civil Service. I started the process with limited enthusiasm but gradually became excited about the graduate scheme working within UK central Government. I finished the thesis for the Masters' degree as rapidly as possible.

In my time living in Bradford, I developed a love of walking and two strong friendships with the men with whom I shared a house, one of whom sadly died 15 years ago after a degenerative illness. In educational terms, Vancouver was a high and Bradford a low. In terms of shaping the next steps in my life journey, both years were crucial.

As a government servant, I soaked up learning from a wide range of leaders nationally and locally. I had an appetite both to learn and to enable others to stretch their aspirations and become braver in what they sought to achieve. A month-long high-potential development programme in 1993 brought me into close contact with leaders in the private sector as well as the public sector. There was a delightful pragmatism among my new colleagues from the private sector which rubbed off on me in the way I approached successive leadership roles.

In my latter years as a director general in government, I spent an increasing amount of time mentoring younger colleagues. It was a natural progression to move into coaching as a second career which included doing an advanced diploma in executive coaching. Since then, I have experienced a regular diet of short, focused programmes on different aspects of coaching skills.

As a coach I needed to hone my skills in the way I listened to the thoughts and emotions behind the words. The presenting issue was not always the issue that needed to be addressed. I needed to develop the way I engaged in dialogue, allowing substantive and deep-seated issues to surface in a natural and open way. This led to the writing of the book *Conversation Matters: how to engage effectively with one another*, which explored the characteristics of conversations that engage, discern and stretch, through chapters that looked at, in turn, listening, encouraging, challenging, short, painful, unresponsive and joyful conversations.

A highlight has been doing a doctorate at Chester University in my early 60s on the theme of 'How leaders step up successfully into demanding leadership roles and sustain that success'. This was a doctorate by publication which involved submitting the books and booklets I had written over a five-year period, plus a critical assessment of what I observed in leaders who had developed an approach that had been sustained successfully during rapid change. This exercise was hugely timely in enabling me to shape my narrative on the mindset we can bring to leading well.

My thesis was that sustaining success at times of rapid change requires coherence, clarity of context, courage and co-creation. Coherence involves being comfortable in yourself as a leader; knowing and living your values; and ensuring personal wholeness. Appreciating your context includes understanding current reality; seeing opportunities; and recognizing moments that matter. Courage involves being willing to do what you believe is right; being willing to step up with conviction; and being deliberate in choosing your attitude. Co-creation requires building effective engagement, creating shared agendas and celebrating outcomes.

Reflections

1. What type of educational approach works best for you at your current stage in life?
2. What are the areas of learning or understanding that you would like to develop further over the next five years?
3. What is a subject that could particularly catch your imagination over the next phase of life?

7 The place of work within life

One of the positive changes in work practices over the early years of the 2020s has been the greater opportunity for flexible working. The dramatic increase in virtual working following Covid-19 has reinforced its acceptance. A growing number of forward-thinking organizations are encouraging a pattern of hybrid working with some days a week in a central workplace and other days working from home.

Another significant development has been the increase in the number of job-share partnerships. My colleague Hilary Douglas and I have done a lot of work with job-shares and together wrote the guide *'Job-sharing: A model for the future workplace?'* in which we explore the benefits of job-sharing for both employers and individuals. The growing number of job-share partnerships are evidencing the benefits for employers of such arrangements as they bring a set of skills, styles, perspectives and experiences unlikely to be found in one person. Successful job-sharers coach and learn from each other with their mutual mentoring reducing the demand on their manager to be a sounding board.

The benefit for job-sharers is principally that they can do interesting, demanding jobs and yet are able to preserve four days of each week for personal and family priorities rather than two. We are seeing an increased variety of job-share partnership arrangements involving both men and women. It is allowing men to play a bigger role in terms of family responsibilities and allowing job-sharers in general to play a bigger role in volunteering in community organizations.

The expectation that the man goes off to work at 7.00a.m. five days a week and is back twelve hours later while the woman stays at home focused on the children is rapidly disappearing, resulting in the need for very deliberate choices about how time is split between work and the rest of life.

With no formal retirement age, the opportunity to work part time in one's 60s and 70s is becoming increasingly feasible and, moreover, is increasingly recognized as more beneficial in terms of both physical and mental health than immediately shifting from full-time work to full-time leisure.

The pattern of working intensively for a number of months and then having a longer break has long been accepted in areas like offshore engineering. Increasingly, this pattern is becoming more accepted in other spheres, including consultancy. The idea of sabbatical has long been a feature of university employment and some church organizations. The pattern of paid or unpaid sabbaticals is becoming increasingly acceptable in a range of different spheres.

There is a much greater opportunity to be deliberate in deciding how work fits in with the rest of life. As you think about shaping your future, it is worth reflecting on what type of opportunities are opening up or could be opened up in your areas of work or interest. You may need to draw examples from sectors other than your own in order to persuade your management to agree to what may seem to them to be novel and risky arrangements.

When Frances and I were first married, I was working long hours as Private Secretary to the Permanent Secretary at the UK Department for Education and Science. Frances worked for a publishing company more locally. My hours became longer when I worked as Principal Private Secretary to a couple of UK Cabinet Ministers. Frances and I accepted this as a way of life as this role was so interesting and a good career opportunity. I am very grateful to Frances for her forbearance when I was working long hours in London for five days each week.

I was completing my stint running the private office of a Cabinet Minister when our first son was born, so the hours became more manageable. I also gave up playing cricket for a village side in order to devote two days at the weekend to the family. I note that in the families of our children the increased scope for home and virtual working has made a big difference in terms of the involvement of parents in the lives of the children. Long may this continue.

When I was given the opportunity to spend two years as the Government Regional Director in the north east of England, it was important that there was a benefit for Frances from that secondment. We relocated to Durham which enabled Frances to do a Masters' degree in the Theology Department at the university. This became the basis for Frances subsequently completing a doctorate and teaching New Testament studies at graduate level.

Spending nearly ten years as a member of the Board of Government Departments involved long hours and lots of reading. Part of each weekend was taken up with office work. At the level I was operating at, there was an inevitability about this level of commitment. I encourage the people I coach to be realistic about the amount of time they will need to put into their work and to seek to break up the work to seek to preserve time for family and community activities.

I ceased being a civil servant when I reached the age of 55. I had no desire to retire and was delighted to start a second career in executive coaching. The hours I work are still equivalent to full time but with more flexibility. My concession to retirement had been to put into the diary more holidays and walking expeditions as fixed points. My hope is to keep coaching for as long as people want me to work with them, and then to seek to move gracefully into the next phase of life.

I am conscious that I am in some ways defined by my work. There is a particular satisfaction for me in going into the study and looking at books which are like old friends. In parallel there is an excitement about working with new people and learning from their life experiences.

Reflections

1. What is the part you want work to play in your life over the next few years?
2. How do significant others in your life view your level of commitment to work?
3. How best do you balance paid employment, voluntary work and family commitment time?

8 Friendships, marriage and children

Friendships used to be maintained by periodic letters, occasional brief phone calls and irregular rendezvous. Rapid developments in information technology have meant that communication is now much easier. Our children have kept in touch with a far wider range of people from their university days than we did because of email and different electronic media. The joy of good friendship is much less about relatively superficial Twitter interactions and much more about occasional meetings and good quality conversation. Maintaining good quality friendships is all the more important in maintaining our well-being when faced with a myriad of uncertainties.

As we look to the future, an important question is, which friendships do we want to develop further? What are the friendships we want to rekindle because they build on special shared memories and are sources of inspiration? What type of time-consuming interchanges on social media do we want to withdraw from because they inhibit development of friendships that are precious and important to us?

Decisions about life partnerships and marriage are as significant as they have ever been. As we live longer, how a married relationship evolves effectively over time as people's interests vary becomes increasingly significant.

The decision whether or not to have children continues to be a key question for many. Adopting children has become increasingly difficult and complicated. As Frances and I move into the next phase of our life, a key factor is what our children most need from us. We like to think that people in their thirties and forties are self-sufficient. But the role of grandparents is perhaps becoming increasingly important as we are living longer and are healthier for longer. When both parents are working there is more demand and even expectation on 'grandparent power' being deployed in childcare.

Frances and I have been good companions since we were married in 1975. A shared interest in walking and travel has been a special delight. Time with children and grandchildren has kept us alert to changing patterns in the contemporary world.

Certain friendships have been very significant over many decades. Dave Martin and I have shared a love of cricket for 60 years and recently walked part of the Thames Path together. Judy Brown stayed at my parents' home during the week when we were both at secondary school: we developed a strong brother/sister-type relationship which has thrived over 60 years. Richard Sattin and Ruth Ackroyd from university days have brought a grounded Sheffield realism to many conversations. Dave Quine was a good friend from Vancouver with whom I have thoughtful conversations about the way leaders make decisions. Judy Hurst and Rob Innes from our time in Durham have always been sources of insight and wisdom.

Hilary Douglas was a colleague in government for over 30 years. She brings a combination of single-mindedness and a wide understanding of the dynamics in any situation. Having worked together in different roles in government, we have been part of the Praesta coaching team for well over a decade and written a number of joint publications. Over the last ten years, Ruth Sinclair has been an important sounding board as I have thought through different coaching approaches and ideas. These friendships have been very significant in providing reflective space as well as numerous prompts and ideas.

Our children have been a huge inspiration. Graham brings insights about people and situations. Ruth is a wonderful encourager and wise in her advice. Colin is a clear, decisive thinker in an understated and influential way. Their spouses, Anna, Owen and Holly, bring their own distinctive, delightful personalities and are wholly committed to the well-being of the whole family. It will be a joy to be involved in the lives of our seven grandchildren for as long as we have the health that enables us to keep up.

There are different decisions and different phases of life that determine how much time is committed to friends, family, work, community and voluntary activities. For me, family is key, but not to the exclusion of other areas of interest and activity. When 100% of someone's time is committed to their family, there is a risk that their horizons become limited and the contribution and spice they can bring into their family life thereby does, to some extent, diminish.

Reflections

1. Which friendships do you particularly want to nurture and grow over the next season?
2. What balance do you put on personal friendships as against professional friendships?
3. How do you want to enhance the relationship with significant others in your life?
4. How do you want to invest your time and energy with the children in your family?

9 Financial priorities

Readers of this book are likely to have more financial choices than many people. A significant proportion of people have no financial reserves. We may complain about costs rising but if we have a regular income and some savings, then we do have choices.

There are financial choices to be made at each stage of life. If there are children in our lives, there are significant costs associated with their upbringing. There are choices about what expenditure is incurred on educational opportunities: for some this will be school fees, but for all parents there are decisions about what sort of trips or clubs are joined. There are choices about housing, travel and gifts to charity. There are decisions on how much to save or what to put in a life assurance scheme. The risk is to set off on one mindset path about the use of finance and not anticipate changes or fail to adapt in response to changing circumstances.

Although the focus of my coaching conversations is usually on someone's contribution in a work context, I periodically invite people to reassess their financial situation and their short- and longer-term priorities. Arguably, accumulating wealth without regard to how it may be dispersed wisely is as irresponsible as accumulating debt without regard to how the debt is going to be ameliorated.

As many of us are living longer there is potentially the opportunity to do a portfolio of activities, some of which are paid and many of which are unremunerated. I have found that the greatest satisfaction often comes from roles where there is no financial return attached.

I was brought up in a household where my parents were very careful with money. In the immediate post-war era money was tight. My father's first priority was to own his own house. He bought his first car when he reached the age of 60, but sadly died a few months later. The legacy of being very careful with money meant that I was even able to save money out of my student grant. I still prefer to drink coffee out of flask sat outside, even if there is the option of a cosy café nearby.

After I began full-time work, the priority was to buy a house within three years, which Frances and I did in Godalming as it was on a fast train line to Waterloo, which was adjacent to the office where I was working. We moved four years later to a home more suitable for a family elsewhere in Godalming where we have lived for over 40 years. Financially, we could have afforded to move to a grander residence but did not want to take on extra financial commitments and wanted to stay in the local community. Now approaching our mid-seventies, we are relieved that we stayed put in suburban Godalming because of the proximity to both the town and the church community we are part of.

I inherited from my father a belief that you balanced economy in day-to-day living with investing in good holidays. As a consequence, we made numerous trips to France, staying in village cottages when the children were small. In their teenage years, we went on family expeditions to places like Vancouver, Toronto, Amsterdam, Paris and the Edinburgh Festival. After a break of a few years, during which the children were not particularly interested in family holidays, we have had a sequence of family trips with our children and their families to places like the Isle of Wight, North Yorkshire, the Lake District, the Chilterns, Wales and different parts of the Cotswolds. Frances and I have regarded investment in family holidays as invaluable in sustaining strong family links at a time when the family were geographically dispersed across the UK.

I was brought up to see giving to charitable organizations as part of investing in the local community and in wider, international priorities. Our focus has been on supporting various educational bodies that we have been linked with, our local church and overseas development organizations. Frances had a long association with Feed the Minds which is a charity that invests in the development of literacy skills in third world countries. Our concern sometimes has been whether some organizations have changed priorities too quickly without due regard to the reasons why charitable gifts were made in the first place.

As an executive coach, I am always happy to buy someone a coffee or a modest meal. I regret that in my first career I was too frugal and did not invest enough in professional relationships at an informal level. My early life and my work in government ensures that now when I invite someone for coffee or a meal, the costs are such that nobody feels embarrassed about receiving hospitality.

As a child, I was worried sometimes that, as part of a single-parent family, the finances would run out. Thankfully, my mother's judicious use of funds meant that we did not reach the edge of any precipice. I am fortunate now not to be at risk financially. I am indebted to my background in terms of being very deliberate that financial resources are not wasted.

Reflections

1. What is the legacy of your upbringing on your attitude to money?
2. What adjustments to the way you spend your financial resources might now be appropriate?
3. To what extent can you increase your giving to charitable organizations?

10 Mistaken directions and disappointments

We all live with regrets. On a long walk we study the map to seek to ensure we keep going on the right track, but there will be moments when we go off course. We may be frustrated because we have lost some time, but we might also have seen a different view which we would have missed if we had kept to the intended route.

When there is a fork in the road, perhaps we have to travel down one leg of the fork for a while before we can judge which is the correct way forward. As we then walk back to the point of intersection, we might be complaining to ourselves of the wasted steps; or we might be delighted that we now know which fork in the road is the correct one.

Some of the best teachers did not choose to become a teacher at the age of 21. They may well have been working in other contexts and gradually recognized that they had an aptitude for teaching. A neighbour locally had a good career in banking but then decided to switch into teaching in their thirties. After a period in the classroom, he became a head teacher and is now Professor of Educational Leadership at a highly respected university. His time working in banking was not wasted: it developed skills in him that have transferred into a new sphere to very good effect.

A scientist will do many experiments before they find the right solution to a problem. They can either describe the experiments that did not work as failures or as valuable learning in finding out that one particular formula was not the right way forward.

If we have taken no mistaken directions, we have very few stories to tell to others about experiences that worked or did not work. We observe in the children in our lives how their days are full of mistaken directions as they learn about their own strengths and the reality of the world around them.

The level of resilience we have is key when there are mistaken directions. What enables us to 'bounce back' when there are setbacks? Sometimes what is needed is commiseration; at other times the best antidote is to do some quick and decisive planning about moving in a different direction. At all times it is an invitation for reflection.

For me, was it a mistake to go straight to Durham University and not pursue Cambridge University as a possibility? No, as the Durham experience was key to my growing up. Should I have agreed to move the family to Durham for two years in order to take up my first director post? The move did have benefits for Frances and enabled me to do the job that I enjoyed most of the 19 I did in my Civil Service career. There were downsides for our children, however, as friendship bonds were broken for a period.

Should I have moved on from the Senior Civil Service at 53 rather than 55? Some of the experiences in the last two years in the Civil Service, which were frustrating, have enabled me to be a better coach as a consequence. Should I have moved on from Praesta Partners when I was frustrated by the governance on a couple of occasions? By staying I have sought to help sustain and develop a healthy coaching business with a new generation of committed and able coaches. I am thrilled that the Praesta coaching business has moved into another phase in providing an energetic contribution to leaders post-Covid.

I could have retired when I was 55, 60, 65 or 70, but have kept working, coaching individuals and teams. Perhaps I could have done more travel and walked more long-distance walks, but the delight in seeing people grow and tackle difficult issues well is so fulfilling.

There are inevitably times when I recall what might have been. If I had stayed in Canada in 1971, what would life have been like and what sort of family would I have been part of? If we had returned to Durham in the mid-2000s, would I have found university life satisfying? If I had gone into management consultancy when I left the Civil Service (where I had a job offer) and not into coaching, what would that experience have been like? Thankfully these questions are curiosities and not regrets.

I am thankful that I have no deep-seated regrets about my life choices. I do recognize that this is not the case for many people whose choices about work, location and relationships have resulted in times and seasons that were less than fulfilling and left a sense of disappointment. In coaching conversations, I encourage people to be honest with themselves about mistaken directions or regrets. I invite them to articulate why they might harbour potential resentments or anguish.

Sometimes talking through these stories can help bring a new understanding. On other occasions, I invite people to tell their story from a different perspective and reflect on how they would advise someone in a similar situation to them. Often the advice they would want to give to others is derived from the learning that came from mistaken directions and how healing and renewal can best take place. I invite them to be honest with themselves and to recognize when previous motivations have now changed. I encourage them to allow time to heal wounds of regret and resentment. I encourage them to think through what a new start involves for them.

Reflections

1. What have been the main lessons gained from mistaken directions?
2. How best do you approach decisions which are like a fork in the road with no obvious clarity about which is the right choice?
3. How best do you advise others who are having to cope with their mistaken choices?

C

Recognize Your Voice and Influence

Often our voice and influence are greater than we might anticipate. Those we are talking with may not look as if they are
listening or may be giving the impression that they disagree
with our stance. We may find a few weeks later that they have
absorbed our point of view and are articulating as their own
view the very thing we had been suggesting weeks earlier.

On other occasions, we may think our voice and influence
are significant but are actually ignored because we have not
caught the mood, or we are regarded as a voice of the past.
Often the most influential voice comes from the person who
speaks briefly at key moments and is able to encapsulate diverse
views and to propose a way forward. Often the most influential
voices come from people who ask the most pertinent questions
and can thereby redirect the thrust of a conversation. Often
influence comes through helping to shape the pace of a conversation so it either slows down to be more reflective, or speeds
up for a greater degree of urgency.

Recognizing your voice starts from knowing your strengths,
celebrating defining moments, shaping your contributions and
being focused on your choices. It also involves an acceptance of
when your influence is limited, and when there is little point in
wasting your breath further.

11 Know your strengths

The good teacher draws out the strengths of every member of the class. The perceptive manager gets to know the strengths of those working with them and develops an understanding of how to draw the best out of all of them.

When I work with teams, I will often invite team members to affirm the particular strengths of their colleagues. On a surprising number of occasions, individuals have not fully appreciated how their strengths are experienced by their colleagues. An individual may take for granted their capacity to put together an argument cogently and do not see this as a particular strength. Their colleagues may admire this quality and want them to deploy it even more often. An individual who is naturally calm does not necessarily appreciate how others find that calmness reassuring, enabling them to feel more at home in making their contributions in discussions.

Using strengths well is linked to not overusing them. An individual who brings the strength of a positive and enthusiastic approach can become overbearing and overwhelming if that strength is deployed to excess.

As you begin to think about the next phase of life, it is worth reassessing which strengths are going to be distinctive and valuable in that next phase. Perhaps you take for granted what could be a unique contribution in a different context. For example, someone who is part of a team that runs complicated processes or systems may feel they are not particularly gifted, but in another context, they bring unique skills that will be greatly valued by less well-structured organizations or charities. Someone employed deep in an accountancy firm may feel they are not particularly gifted; in another organization they may well find their financial skills are hugely valued and sought after.

Officials working in central or local government may feel they are not qualified to do roles outside government organizations. My constant message to them is that their training in government organizations has helped them to bring objective reasoning about pros and cons, a deep understanding of how politicians think and act, an ability to be dispassionate and set out practical forward steps, and an ability to synthesize arguments to bring out key differentiating points.

When I began work in the Civil Service, I felt there was a bit of a chip on my shoulder. I had gone to a local state school, grown up in financially tight circumstances and came from a small, parochial Yorkshire coastal town. Over time I recognized that my background gave me particular strengths: it was helpful to have been shaped by a northern upbringing where finances were tight. I think this tendency to frugality made me a better Treasury official and Finance Director General than I would have been if I had been brought up with plenty of spare cash around.

I had been a shy, unconfident child with continuing echoes of impostor syndrome as a young graduate civil servant. What greatly helped was the belief that my seniors had in me in those first few years working in a government department. Hugh Jenkins, Donald King, John Hudson, Sheila Browne and Edward Simpson affirmed me and reinforced a growing confidence.

In my latter years as a Director General, I thoroughly enjoyed mentoring individuals moving into new roles. I was asked by the Cabinet Office to work with a couple of new recruits into senior roles in the Civil Service. Because of the feedback I received, I increasingly felt that moving into coaching as a second career would be something I would enjoy: using gifts others said I had to enable people to see possibilities ahead.

For a few years, I was glad not to be in an overall leadership role as I sought to learn the skills of an executive coach. But in more recent times, I have been happy to chair both Praesta Partners and Guildford Cathedral Council. I get a peculiar satisfaction out of structuring meetings so that they are as productive as possible, including ensuring that the timekeeping is effective.

There is always scope to keep on developing our skills. In the book *Thriving in your Work*, I delighted in exploring the skill of forgetting. The more we forget, the more room there is in our brains to absorb and enjoy new emotions and insights. Sometimes our brains are so cluttered with past beliefs, loyalties and burdens that we need a clean break from the emotions that have captured and debilitated us.

My encouragement to those I work with is to recognize and own their strengths and then to put themselves in situations where those strengths can be deployed in ways that will both give personal satisfaction and help create constructive change.

Reflections

1. What are the strengths that others see in you that you don't necessarily fully appreciate?
2. What strengths have become increasingly apparent in recent years?
3. When are there risks of your overusing your strengths?
4. Where might we apply the skill of forgetting?

12 Celebrate defining moments

I have recently read a biography by Brenda Hale entitled *Spider Woman: a Life*. Brenda Hale was the first female President of the UK Supreme Court. As a young girl from a little village in North Yorkshire, she only went into Law because her head teacher told her she was not clever enough to study history. She became the most senior judge in the UK following an unconventional path to the top. In the forethoughts to the book, she describes four imposter moments; she then describes how she learnt to cope with impostor moments. These were defining moments that enabled her to have the courage and confidence to take the lead on hugely controversial cases.

In the book *The Prime Ministers We Never Had*, Steve Richards describes defining moments in the lives of ten senior UK politicians when choices were made in favour of others at key moments. When I wrote the book *Defining Moments: navigating through business and organizational life*, I explored the significance for leaders of 'light going on' moments, milestone moments and surprising moments. I reflect in the book on surviving difficult moments, treasuring good moments, capturing creative moments. Under the theme of treasuring moments,

I reflected on how different leaders had made each moment matter, had accepted the truth of hard messages and embedded learning moments.

Enabling people to explore key defining moments in their personal and professional journeys has proved to be a rich area of exploration. I invite individuals and teams to stand back after both joyful and difficult moments to reflect on how such moments have shaped their character and their perspective about the future.

The foreword to the book *Defining Moments* was written by Lesley Strathie who began work in the most junior grade in government as a temporary administrative assistant and ended up as the Head of the UK Revenue and Customs Department (HMRC). Lesley describes key defining moments when people believed in her. She had to seize the moment when she was asked to step into the role of Acting Chief Executive of Jobcentre Plus: she immediately fully occupied the role as the person in charge.

When Lesley was hesitant about becoming Head of the UK Revenue and Customs Department, we had lengthy conversations about the pros and cons of such a step. She wrote in her Foreword that 'I absorbed her hesitancy.' She wrote that Peter's 'quizzical look when I was not sure I wanted to be considered for the job was part of the process of switching my attitude to a role which I now thoroughly enjoy'. Sadly, Lesley's time at HMRC was limited as cancer took its grip when her work there was only partly done.

One of the joys of coaching leaders is enabling them to recognize and shape defining moments. In the reflective space provided by a coaching conversation there is scope for leaders to recognize key moments on their journey and then explore and affirm their next steps.

I look back on various personal defining moments, starting with going to Durham University, then to Regent College, Vancouver and then joining the UK Civil Service. I remember being firmly reprimanded by Mark Carlisle, the Education Secretary of State, while I was his private secretary. I must have been complaining about something when he said to me, 'You are one of the grown-ups now. You need to recognize that you have an influential voice.' This direct comment brought me up short: it was a very pertinent observation. I needed to recognize that I would be listened to and, when I needed to voice an opinion, need not hold back. The fact that I was a northern lad from a single-parent family was in no way a detriment.

Moving to work in the UK Treasury was a defining moment as it opened up a much wider perspective across the Government. As a Treasury Deputy Director I had a direct line to the Chief Secretary of the Treasury (the Cabinet Minister leading on how public expenditure was allocated) and on occasions, to the Chancellor of the Exchequer.

Becoming the Government Regional Director for the North-east of England was a defining moment in terms of authority and influence. This was in the early 1990s before email or video communication, hence we could operate very much at arm's length from Whitehall. Following the riots in Meadow Well and Newcastle in 1992, we had to act quickly in partnership with a wide range of private, public and voluntary organizations to respond to underlying unease and tensions. Having the opportunity to put a stamp on the city challenge initiatives and develop coordinated responses was much more satisfying than the arm's length influence I had as a senior official in Whitehall.

In 2001 I spent a weekend at a conference in Cambridge and met an executive coach for the first time. We had a good conversation over tea which inspired me to think that coaching could be something I would enjoy and feel fulfilled doing. It was two years later before the initial thought about coaching turned into reality, but my wife Frances felt, right from the moment I told her of the conversation in Cambridge, that moving into executive coaching would be the eventual outcome.

When I moved into coaching, an immediate area of engagement was helping to lead a programme called Pathways which was designed for individuals with potential from ethnic minority backgrounds. It was a shock to see how assumptions made both by individuals and organizations had held back the progress of talented people. It was a delight to see how participants on the programme grew in confidence, with a number going on to high-profile roles, such as Baljit Ubhey at the Crown

Prosecution Service. I have had the privilege of working with a wide range of leaders from ethnic minorities who have made outstanding contributions in their respective spheres.

In terms of personally defining moments, I recall vividly, aged 7, sitting on my mother's knee and being told my father had died. There was a resulting numbness in my emotions for a few years. Meeting Frances in Toronto in 1973 was a defining moment which has led to a special companionship over the last 50 years. The birth of three children and the arrival of seven grandchildren have been moments of very special delight, joy and celebration.

I encourage people to write down their defining moments and talk about them. Allowing defining moments to shape your future gives a foundation for next steps. I keep suggesting that defining moments are not just events of the past: there will be more defining moments as the future unfolds.

Reflections

1. What are the defining moments that are most special for you, both professionally and personally?
2. Are there defining moments that you haven't fully acknowledged which it would be good to share with others? Who might you share one of those defining moments with?
3. How best do you approach the prospect of future defining moments as you shape the next steps on your journey?

13 Shape your contributions

In 2012, I was laid low with a detached retina. I had been in discussion with a publisher about writing a book on personal impact and gained their agreement for me to write the book during the two-week period when I had to sit still and not move following the operation that sealed the detached retina back in place. Dictating a book was an ideal way of keeping my head still and avoiding boredom.

In that book I explored how to build influence, talking about the different dos and don'ts of being influential. That book was followed up by a sequence of books with each one setting out 100 ideas on separate themes, namely: Coaching, Team Effectiveness, Building Success, Leading Well, Handling Rapid Change and Leading Through Frustration. The thrust of each of the books was about owning your contribution and being deliberate in how you respond to external factors and how you chart a forward course, which enables you to make a distinctive and influential contribution. When writing these books, I have been reminding myself of what is most important and have sought to write clear, concise and practical prose.

In coaching conversations, we are often exploring the distinctiveness of the 'value-add' someone brings as a leader. Visual images are often helpful, like the difference between steering and rowing. There may be moments when you need to row, but the leader's prime objective is often to steer a way forward. There are moments when a leader needs to define the vision going forward, but often they are shaping a vision, drawing on the perspective of all those who have an interest. The more senior someone becomes, the more the leadership role revolves around enabling, empowering, encouraging and elucidating. There may be blockages that need to be addressed or difficult relationships that need to be changed round.

Often, the question that helps to clarify someone's essential, distinctive contribution is, 'What is it only you can do in this leadership role?' It is the coaching question that has been most powerful in helping people unlock their personal priorities: it is often the question that they later describe as having been central to the shaping of their decisions about their leadership contribution.

In our book *Business Coaching: achieving practical results through effective engagement*, my then colleague Robin Linnecar and I set out what we saw as the golden thread running through effective engagement between coach and client, namely:

- Respect, involving trust and mutual support
- Listening, being fully present and giving undivided attention
- Open-minded in banishing pre-conceived notions
- Flexible in varying the approach, pace and timing
- Supportive in encouragement and emphasizing the positive
- Challenging in creating a context where frank exchange can happen, and
- Forward-looking with a relentless focus on the future.

When I work with emerging leaders, I will often draw from five key axes I set out in the Praesta Insight booklet, *Living Leadership: finding equilibrium*. This refers to the balance between: leading and managing, short-term and long-term, the individual and the team, activity and reflection, and being resolute and adaptable. Leaders need to find the right equilibrium in all these axes with the right position varying over time. I encourage them to think about the balance between their leadership and management responsibilities. Good leadership ignites a passion to make a difference and inspires followers. Sound management is about a well-planned programme, project performance and risk management. It requires clear expectations on outcomes and standards, linked with a significant degree of empowerment.

Recognizing the urgent alongside the important is about the necessity of keeping the show on the road while delivering the transformation necessary to achieve long-term goals. There are moments when the leader has to act alone and times when it is all about enabling the team to succeed.

Getting the equilibrium right between activity and reflection is about connecting heart and head, bringing focus and observation, and applying determination and detachment. A significant element in coaching conversations is about getting this balance right. Setting aside dedicated time for reflection is never straightforward in busy roles but essential for long-term survival and progress. A persistent coaching theme is working out that 'sweet spot' when time for reflection will be most rejuvenating and productive.

Being resolute and adaptable is perhaps the toughest balance to achieve. Being resolute is about having the passion to make a difference in uncertain times and a doggedness to keep at it. Being adaptable and agile involves recognizing when persistent action and determination can risk blinkering our understanding of current reality.

Looking forward, we can potentially shape our contributions and need not be captive to how we have done things in the past. Many of our offers to contribute looking forward may be turned down, but we may be surprised by the influence we can have over time when we are judicious and deliberate in the way we seek to contribute.

In my first two jobs in the Civil Service, I was a single operator doing tasks in response to particular remits. The big shift was going into private office to be private secretary to the Head of Department where a key role was to be the bridge or interpreter between him and the rest of the organization. I had to give clear steers about what was needed. I was the eyes and ears of the Permanent Secretary; I had to pick up and understand concerns and feed back the learning in a constructive way. Subsequently working as Principal Private Secretary for a particularly demanding Secretary of State, Sir Keith Joseph, reinforced the need to become a trusted interpreter between Ministers and officials.

As Press Secretary to two Secretaries of State, I knew that my words would often appear in the media as 'A spokesmen said ...'. I knew that I had to be ultra-careful that my contributions were accurate, credible and would not cause embarrassment.

When negotiating with the Treasury about the budget for the Education and Employment Department, I knew I needed to craft my words carefully and know when I had to be robust and when I could negotiate. It became second nature to talk to some key people in advance before shaping any interventions. I always regarded people like Nick Stuart and Leigh Lewis as excellent barometers of what arguments would work or not work in particular negotiations.

As an executive coach, I am conscious that it is never for me to tell someone what to do. I must never be directive, but I have a responsibility to ensure that the conversations focus on the right topics with the right questions being addressed. I readily admit that I frequently ask leading questions that seek to draw from my understanding of what is happening and help focus discussion, so that the individual or the team can explore next steps in a poignant way and reach outcomes that they feel are considered and sustainable.

As the Chair of the Guildford Cathedral Council, I have a responsibility to ensure that the right topics are considered by this advisory body. It is for the Cathedral Chapter, who are the trustees under both ecclesiastical and charity law, to make the decisions. My remit is to shape the contribution of the Council so that there is proper, informed conversation about strategy and finance, with the Chapter having the benefit of dialogue within the Council as an input into their decisions on next steps.

My constant refrain in coaching is to encourage people to shape the way they contribute, so that they are influential in a way that enables others to fulfil their responsibilities to best effect. I will often pose the question in coaching conversations, 'If you were bold, what would you do?' This prompts a conversation about what might be possible. There are a number of occasions when that question has been put to me and it has opened up possibilities that I had previously shied away from.

Reflections

1. When have your contributions been most influential and why was that?
2. How wide is your repertoire in terms of the way you make contributions?
3. What do you see as areas where you can further develop and shape the way you influence?
4. If you were bold, what would you do next?

14 Be focused in your decisions

The most effective chairs of meetings provide scope for all participants to contribute and then ensure that there is enough time at the end of a meeting to clearly set out the conclusions, ensuring that the note taker or the person taking the lead following the meeting has understood and accepted the conclusions. A confident chair may well ask someone else in advance to be the person who summarizes at the end of a discussion, with the chair then having the opportunity to clarify the conclusions if needed and check that there is assent to next steps.

This does not mean that decisions need to be reached prematurely. Often the appropriate conclusion of a meeting is that further information is needed on particular aspects, or the views of affected individuals need to be sought before conclusions can be reached. I always thought there was particular merit in the UK parliamentary arrangements whereby a second reading debate would preface the detailed scrutiny of proposals in a Bill at the Committee stage. I found it a useful shorthand to suggest having a 'second reading' discussion on a particular topic to gauge people's overall perspectives, before getting into detail in subsequent focused conversations.

Soon after moving into coaching, I had a sequence of conversations with leaders in different spheres about how they made decisions. My consultees included senior leaders in the Judiciary, the Bank of England, NATO, the UK Government, education, business, diplomacy and prisons, as well as chief constables, government Ministers, charity chief executives and bishops. What came out of this research were four themes about good decision-making, covering:

- Clarity: utter objectivity about the issue, the context and the consequences
- Conviction: the place of intuition and trained judgement
- Courage: turning belief into action to build next steps
- Communication: embracing listening, engaging and persuading.

The way leaders balance clarity and conviction is critical. Bringing clarity is about focusing on key facts and the main objectives, ensuring that options are clear, that the risks have been identified and the nature of success defined. Conviction is about drawing on past experience about the likelihood of success and assessing whether the capability is there to implement decisions effectively. Conviction is about drawing on intuitive perceptions which flow from previous experience. It involves weighing up options against the values that are most important as touchstones in the decisions. It may well be that there are overwhelming facts that mean the intuitive sense is not relevant but cross-checking the assessment of facts with your intuitive sense is always useful in helping settle on whether the conclusions are in the right direction. I sought to crystallize these themes in the book *Making Difficult Decisions* and the subsequent short book entitled *Deciding Well* which included a theological reflection on decision making.

When thinking about the next step on your leadership journey, it is always worth seeking clarity about the different options, observing the inner convictions that flow to the surface, recognizing whether there is the courage internally to move into unknown territory, and then thinking through how you would communicate your decision in a way that convinces family, friends and colleagues.

When I spent two years in the UK Government Treasury, I worked directly for Nick Monck, an energetic Director General. We worked together on employment policy and on introducing profit-related pay: this was intended as a temporary measure that stayed in place for 20 years. Nick was brilliant in engaging Ministers and leaders both in business and across Whitehall. He was exemplary in ensuring there were clear, precise summaries at the end of meetings. I learnt a lot from observing him and other leaders who acted with precision when that was needed.

When I was negotiating with the Treasury as a Finance Director General in Education and Employment, it was important to get to conclusions eventually but not to rush at those conclusions. The one occasion when I lost my cool in a telephone conversation with the Treasury was when my interlocutor (Nick Holgate) was being entirely unreasonable in not allowing a decision to be reached. In a fleeting burst of anger, I threw a 'worry ball' across my office, creating a dint in the wall opposite. Thankfully, this was a subject that Nick and I could laugh about in subsequent years. When I moved on from the Finance role, I presented Nick with the worry ball as a reminder of our frank and normally productive engagement.

As you explore next steps on your leadership journey, it is helpful to be clear on the decisions you need to make and the criteria which will be relevant in making those decisions. Writing down those criteria gives a point of reference against which different options can be assessed.

Not long after I moved into coaching, I was asked by the head of a government department if I would lead an enquiry. I had no hesitation declining the invitation. I was flattered to be asked, but I had moved on emotionally and my heart and mind were in a different place. Sometimes we can surprise ourselves by the clarity of our reactions when we have moved into the next phase of life.

When individuals are exploring different possibilities about their next steps, I invite them to imagine the joys and frustrations of different options. Allowing themselves to sit in an option for a couple of days can help draw out the realities of what will engage them or sap their energy. When they wake up in the morning, are they excited by the possibilities?

When I was thinking seriously about moving on from the Civil Service, I was in the last two for a couple of roles outside government. I was enthusiastic in the final interviews but was not convinced that either role was right for me. There was an inner relief on both occasions when the answer was no. I was thankful that I avoided having to decide whether to accept the role or not. In retrospect my heart was telling me that neither option was right for me. When the route to coaching opened up, there was no hesitation is saying yes to that avenue.

When facing a life decision, I encourage individuals to take their time and talk with significant others in their lives. Decisions about life choices rarely have to be made in a rush. There is nearly always time to talk through pros and cons with trusted others. It is well worth imagining yourself having taken different decisions and reflecting on what would be the joys and frustrations of different options.

It is worth reflecting on how you can sit lightly to different decisions, recognizing that not every decision will turn out as you had hoped. If 75% of your decisions turn out to be good ones, then you are doing well. Sometimes we have to accept that one route proved to be mistaken, that decisions have to be re-evaluated and new choices made.

Reflections

1. Who are your decision-making role models who can weigh up factors well and reach considered decisions?
2. What helps you balance clarity and conviction so that the decisions you make are thought through and sustainable?
3. In respect of forthcoming decisions, what are the principles that will guide the way you make decisions?
4. How best do you sit lightly to decisions that proved to be suboptimal?

15 Accept when your influence is limited

You may have ambitious plans for the contribution you would like to make but your suggestions seem to fall on deaf ears. You learn to bide your time and modify your suggestions in light of what you have heard and begin to gain limited traction.

Perhaps you have been part of an organization or venture for a while and are conscious of past mistakes. Others come in with new enthusiasm who seem to want to explore the same possibilities that did not work last time. You are in a dilemma: do you refer to past debacles or do you identify some of the opportunities and risks which draw from your previous experience without referring directly to past events?

Or you may have worked hard on putting together a set of proposals, having engaged with a range of different interests.

You know how people are likely to respond and yet a more dominant voice is holding sway. You are conscious that your traction is limited. You have made your points and perhaps it is now time to withdraw.

There will be occasions when you want your influence to be limited. It is in the best interest of reaching sustainable outcomes that those more directly affected than you decide. Your role then is to ask key questions or to make some points of principle. You want to help shape the way decisions are made, leaving others to make the decisions. As an advisor or non-executive, you want your influence to be limited so that the accountability for decisions and next steps is clear.

When you consider future possible roles, you have the freedom to shape how you respond, but whether any of the avenues open up will depend on other people's decisions and not yours. Accepting the reality of a 'no' is not always straightforward if we have a strong sense of conviction that a particular forward avenue is the right one.

There were three occasions in my first career when I lost my job: when a new Secretary of State wanted to bring their previous Press Secretary with them; when the Education and Employment Departments were combined and there was only going to be one HR Director for the new Department; and when the decision was taken to bring a University Vice Chancellor onto the Executive Board of the Education Department which meant that my post was abolished.

On each occasion I had no influence on the decision, but there was the opportunity to influence what happened next. On each occasion, after an initial reaction of intense disappointment, I soon recognized that there was no point being grumpy. I needed to see opportunity beyond the disappointment. When I left the Press Secretary role, I volunteered to take the lead in rejuvenating a policy area that was making slow progress in which I then became fully absorbed. In retrospect I was relieved not to become the HR Director for the combined Department in 1995 as the change in direction for me opened up the possibility a year later of becoming the Finance Director.

The restructuring of the Executive Board of the Education

Department in 2003 led to the possibility of a secondment to a coaching organization which led naturally into the second career of executive coaching. It was an example of positive consequences flowing from initially unwelcome decisions made by others. What was important was seeking to maintain a positive frame of mind, that good could come out of initial disappointment. What was key was the attempt to focus beyond the immediate, which was not always straightforward.

I was advised that the coaching organization I should seek to join in 2003 was The Change Partnership. My initial approaches were rebuffed until I was able to mention the possibility of an initial secondment. I was persistent and eventually a short-term secondment was agreed. In one sense I moved from being in influential Director General roles within the Government to a temporary appointment at a small business. In another sense I had begun my next phase of life unencumbered by previous pressures and expectations. There was an excitement about the next opportunity.

The existing coaches at Change Partnership all had their own rooms in the organization's offices. I had to occupy an empty desk wherever I could find one. I was starting up the public sector practice within Change Partnership which had previously focused, almost exclusively, on the private sector. I was able to establish a good number of coaching assignments fairly quickly and was appointed as a full member of the team. I did not push to have a significant influence on the business in the early years as I wanted to build up my coaching practice. Eventually, I succumbed to chairing Praesta Partners and delighted in helping to ensure that the business would develop and be sustainable with new colleagues taking on more of the leadership responsibilities over time.

I have been a Licensed Lay Minister in the Anglican Church for 50 years. I have seen my role as being a bridge between the Church and the work environment. It has been a joy seeking to bring insights into the church context from the work environment, and into the work context from Christian insight and wisdom. On the other hand, I have been deliberate in not getting involved in church administration after a not-very-satis-fying period as a member of the London Diocesan Synod.

Frances has been heavily involved as a church warden in two spells over a total of 13 years. We were deliberate in each having our own separate spheres of influence in the local church context. Mine was more informal through conversation and mentoring alongside leading and speaking at services. Frances' contribution was more directly in governance and leading a particular congregation. That has been a happy balance for both of us, although church dynamics can be even more frustrating than working with politicians. We have felt a strong sense of mutual support in our different contributions to church life locally and nationally.

Sometimes you can be surprised by the influence you have had. A brief piece of advice may stick with someone and then be played back to you years later. One of the joys of coaching work is when someone refers to a seminal conversation a decade earlier which has helped shape their future thinking and decisions.

Reflections

1. When has limited influence frustrated you and how have you handled that?
2. What type of influence, going forward, is most important for you?
3. In what areas of life do you want to be deliberate in minimizing the influence you bring?

D

Recognize the Shadow You Cast

We all cast a shadow, whether we like it or not. We may feel we are just observing but our presence will influence the way others engage. The shadow may be a result of past comments or the reputation we bring. It might be a consequence of what we stand for or are assumed to stand for.

The way we respond in different situations will be mirrored by others. When you bring energy and a positive approach, that is likely to be reflected in the perspective of those we are working with. If our shadow is one of gloom, that is equally likely to seep through and lead to a mood of gloom.

This section considers a number of situations where the shadow we cast will have a cascade effect. It might be situations where challenges need to be gripped or teams influenced. It might be about learning from feedback or taking measured risks. How best we face into the unexpected will inevitably cascade into how others deal with the unpredictable.

16 Take ownership of challenges whether or not they are welcome

If our work and lives contain no challenges, life becomes boring, dull and flat. If there are too many challenges, some of which look insurmountable, then our energy can feel sapped before we begin to address even the first challenge. It is worth reflecting on the number of challenges you feel you can readily handle at the same time.

If there are challenges related to work, family and health

concurrently, you can feel a sense of no escape. If one of the three areas is in a reasonable equilibrium, then we can perhaps handle the churn more easily in the other two. Looking ahead, it is worth reflecting on the mix of challenges in different areas of life that you feel comfortable in addressing simultaneously. You may not want to be moving house and changing jobs at the same time as major family events. Sometimes a cacophony of events might risk overwhelming us. One good friend had to cope with moving house twice, moving jobs twice, living in three different parts of her country alongside the death of her father and caring for her mother, within a two-year period. She kept remarkably cheerful throughout, kept going through conversations with good friends and her Christian faith.

When I was a post graduate student at Regent College in Vancouver, the then Principal (Jim Houston) suggested that I write a book on freedom and responsibility. I was only 21 at the time and thought this idea was unrealistic. As a civil servant for 32 years, I wrote a lot in other people's names but never conceived of writing a book of my own. As a coach in my second career, I had an opportunity to write in my own name and had logged in the back of my mind that one day I would write on the themes of freedom and responsibility.

When visiting Vancouver in 2016, I reminded Jim Houston of what he had said to me 45 years earlier. His comment was, 'Well, it is about time you wrote the book.' As a dutiful former student, I thought I ought to rise to that challenge and hence the writing of the book, *Leadership to the Limits: balancing freedom and responsibility*, which was published 50 years after Jim Houston's initial suggestion.

This was an example of a challenge that had laid dormant for 45 years and did not come to fruition until 50 years after the initial challenge. The thesis in the book was about the importance of embracing freedom and living out responsibility as a joy and not a burden. I was conscious that the shadow we cast when we inhabit our responsibilities is important in ensuring good governance, enabling people to live with expectations, avoiding the blame game and bringing clarity about where the red lines are.

As a Director General, I was conscious that advice needed to be given to Ministers quickly on controversial issues. When I was the Finance Director General, calculations needed to be done at speed. The shadow I tried to cast was that which gave the experts time to do the calculations and then to ensure they were presented carefully, in such a way that their implications were clear. The challenge was to be both calm and decisive at the same time. When working in the Treasury, I was the intermediary balancing the Treasury focus on financial discipline with the never-ending demands and expectations of spending departments.

There was one occasion when a key part of a financial calculation was not done accurately and was not discovered when checked. I had moved onto a different role, but when the problem surfaced three months later, I had a personal conversation with David Blunkett as Secretary of State explaining what had happened and apologizing. To his great credit, he was gracious in his response. Many politicians I worked with handled big issues and problems calmly but often got frustrated on smaller issues.

When I was Government Regional Director in the Northeast of England in 1992, following the riots in Meadow Well and West Newcastle, Michael Heseltine asked to visit the area and meet groups of local people. He wanted to appear incognito so he could meet local people without any local, political or press presence. We set up an event in Meadow Well on the basis that local people would be meeting me. We had kept the forthcoming visit quiet and Michael Heseltine was not spotted coming off the flight in Newcastle.

We arrived in Meadow Well with no police escort. Michael Heseltine then had an open conversation with local people, listening intently to what they said. He gave a speech that afternoon in Newcastle in which he drew on what he had heard on the visit. I was then heavily criticized by local politicians for arranging this clandestine visit to Meadow Well. It so happened that the local politician who was most vociferous in his criticism of what I had facilitated then became a Minister of State in the Education Department five years later where I worked for him relatively closely. Even though he had strongly criticized my action in 1992, our interchange had built a level of respect that underpinned the good working relationship five years later.

When my elder son, Graham, and I wrote a Grove book entitled *Leading in Demanding Times*, Graham was drawing from his experience as a church leader and I was drawing from both my leadership roles and the coaching work. We based our advice around the four themes of attitude, approach, actions and awareness of risks. The elements were:

- Attitude: bring an attitude of humility and keep a wide perspective
- Approach: deal carefully with your emotions and draw on your wisdom and that of others around you
- Actions: be aware of the impact of your words and actions, and be willing to make clear, considered decisions
- Awareness of risks: watch out for power going to your head and watch out for being caught off guard.

These steers have proved to be apt in a wide range of contexts with leaders at a variety of levels.

Reflections

1. What have you noticed about the shadow you have cast when you have taken ownership of a difficult issue?
2. How best do you keep a calm and purposeful demeanour when dealing with an unwelcome challenge that is frustrating you?
3. When has the shadow you cast in dealing with an unwelcome issue been unhelpful and what did you learn from that experience?

17 Influence teams you are part of

It is important never to underestimate the influence you can have on any team you are part of. When you are new to a team and observing, you are influencing the way points are made as other team members will be conscious that they have to present their case in a way that enables a new team member to understand the issues and possibilities. The innocent questions you ask may be far more perceptive than you realize. The new participant in a team can often identify key issues that have not been properly considered or have only been addressed to a very limited extent.

When Hilary Douglas and I reviewed what characterized resilient teams and wrote the booklet *The Resilient Team*, we noticed that teams that stayed resilient:

• Know what the team is for, and what can only be done by the team acting together
• Balance planning the longer term and dealing with the here and now
• Work together to turn plans into reality
• Are proactive in responsive to a changing environment
• Pay attention to values and behaviours
• Engage effectively with stakeholders
• Build capability for sustainable change in the organization
• Understand and apply effective governance
• Maintain momentum as team members change
• Look after their well-being.

When you join a team, these characteristics provide good lenses through which to assess the quality of engagement of the team and how you might most effectively contribute going forward.

Being an authoritative team member means knowing what the leader wants and where you can contribute. It involves recognizing the constraints upon you and how best to be influential. When coaching teams, I encourage them to reflect on what is the particular contribution they want to bring to the team and how they draw the best out of each other. When seeking to influence a team, I have found it helpful to use the framework of the four Vs, posing questions like:

- What is our vision of what the team needs to deliver and how do we want this team to be described by those affected by its work?
- What values will help guide the way we operate and make decisions as a team going forward?
- What is the intrinsic value-add that we can each make to the team's endeavour?
- How do we, as a team, maintain vitality, freshness, openness and curiosity?

When I was a Government Regional Director, I was told I brought a constructive focus which helped me feel increasingly confident in dealing with a range of different topics in which I had had limited previous experience. The feedback when I was a member of the Department of Education Board was that I delivered what I said I would deliver. When I became a member of Michael Bichard's Executive Board at the Department for Education and Employment from 1996 to 2000, I was described by Michael Bichard as the 'glue'. I initially did not know whether to take this comment as a compliment or criticism.

The leadership team included a number of impressive characters, three of whom went on to become permanent secretaries or chief executives, and two others who were very close to being appointed as heads of government departments. My role as Director General for Finance was to chart a way through potential difficulties and ensure outcomes were reached which each team member could own. Being the 'glue' was a role that came naturally by virtue of my preferences and the requirements flowing from being the Finance Director General.

Michael Bichard's successor, David Normington, was an admirable leader who was generous in his support of colleagues. With new members of the leadership team, it became a more competitive environment in which I felt less at home and was, therefore, a less effective contributor. I am indebted to

David for paving the way for me to move on from government into coaching which enabled me to fulfil personal aspirations, and enabled the leadership of the Department for Education and Skills to move on to its next phase.

I learnt a huge amount from some non-executive director roles. As a governor of Godalming College for twelve years, I saw the benefit of an external group of people bringing a wider perspective, able to ask probing questions and bring a longer-term dimension and understanding of the broader community. As a member of the Council of Newcastle University, I relished the opportunity to seek to link national and regional perspectives.

As a governor of St John's College at Durham University, I was part of the appointment of two successive college principals. I learnt a lot from the first appointment where, in retrospect, there was a mismatch between the aspirations of the individual and the needs of the college which we had failed to fully probe in the recruitment process. When it came to the appointment of a successor seven years later, there was a far more rigorous recruitment process which led to the outstanding appointment of David Wilkinson. In over a decade at the college, he has brought a clear sense of forward vision and commitment. He has dealt with complicated staffing issues with skill and sensitivity.

I learnt the importance of how to best support leaders as a non-executive through being available to have conversations at key moments and ensuring that the conclusions of Governing Council meetings were unambiguous. Having to focus my contribution as a non-executive director based on limited time and knowledge helped me become a better executive director. I encourage all the leaders I work with to have some concurrent responsibility in a different sphere to provide complementary learning to their day job.

Reflections

1. How do you describe the shadow you have cast on teams you have been part of?
2. When your role has been non-executive rather than executive, how best have you influenced the decisions made?
3. What role are you best suited to in influencing teams going forward?

18 Learn from feedback

We can be casting a shadow without realizing its full impact. We can be impeding progress or inhibiting others without realizing we are having a detrimental effect. We can believe we know what is right based on our past experiences and want to keep pressing a point of view without fully appreciating how we may be becoming counterproductive. Inviting open feedback at an early stage can help reduce the risk of more abrupt reactions at a later stage.

Receiving feedback when you are well established in a role can be very valuable in informing how best you approach your next phase of leadership. Some of the most effective leaders I know have had a clear commitment to learn from feedback. Gus O'Donnell, when he was Head of the UK Civil Service, used to describe feedback as the most valuable gift you can give someone. Many organizations now include feedback exercises on an annual basis.

Feedback says as much about the giver of the feedback as the recipient of the feedback; hence feedback needs to be viewed with care. What matters is whether there are consistent themes that need attention. Often, the key learning from feedback is about the importance of clear explanation and communication in order to reduce the risk of misunderstanding.

I have worked with Bishop Alan Smith since 2005, initially when he was Bishop of Shrewsbury and then following his becoming Bishop of St Albans. We enjoyed writing the book together, *The Reflective Leader: standing still to move forward*, in which we talked about how best you can know yourself, understand others, create a flourishing team and read the context. We concluded the book by talking about what happens when you stand and stare, what lights your fire and who your companions are on the way.

Alan and I wrote 16 chapters each and then gave feedback to each other in a frank way. We then amended each other's texts in such a way that it was not possible to identify which sections we each originally wrote. The feedback was given frankly and cheerfully around Alan Smith's kitchen table. We had agreed in advance that we could veto each other's proposed wording if we did not agree with it. The principle was that both of us needed to be fully in agreement with everything included in the final text of the book.

Frances was a source of teasing and encouragement as she regarded both of us as activists rather than reflectors and found it amusing that we were writing a book on the reflective leader. Our justification was that because the feedback to both of us had been that we are activists by nature, we were still learning how to reflect. We were not exemplars of reflection, we were learning.

In the first half of my Civil Service career, I was working in areas where I needed to think and act quickly. The strategic expectations were less dominant than the operational requirements. I was regarded as someone who could fix difficult problems and was, therefore, placed in a series of high-profile, demanding roles. The strategic muscle had not been fully developed. As a Director dealing with controversial schools issues, I needed to think ahead more acutely. I received feedback from time to time that my strengths were dealing with Ministers on a day-to-day basis but that I could sometimes bring a more strategic lens.

I don't think that I took full notice of those comments and risked keeping a relentless focus on the day-to-day; hence in my coaching work, I often encourage people to be very deliberate in how they balance the long term and the short term. I encourage people to always think ahead about the skills they need to develop for the future and the type of experiences that will allow them to become more strategic in their leadership approach. The value and positive impact of sincere constructive feedback, humbly received, reflected upon and incorporated into future action, should not be underestimated.

Personally, the feedback from my family is that sometimes I am not fully present and can appear preoccupied. I am conscious that the effect of immediately available communication means we are constantly disturbed. I recognize that I need to turn the iPhone off more often and ensure that I fully focus on the needs of family members. However confronting the feedback is, I am conscious that I need to take it seriously because of the shadow I can cast.

Reflections

1. When has feedback been a significant gift that has influenced your thinking and actions?
2. What inhibits you from seeking feedback?
3. How will recent feedback influence the way you approach the next steps on your leadership journey?

19 Make measured choices

Every day you will make a choice about your attitude of mind in that day. We choose whether to view something that goes wrong as a disaster or failure or as something we have learnt valuable lessons from. If we get 75% of our choices right, we are doing well.

A book I wrote in 2013, which I keep coming back to and use regularly with new people I am working with, is *Getting the Balance Right: leading and managing well*. It is not about how we balance the use of time within any particular day. It covers the balance between areas like following and leading, engagement and detachment, principle and pragmatism. As individuals take on more responsibilities or move into new roles, they do not have the detailed knowledge to make all the decisions. If they try to make all the decisions alone, they are doomed to failure. What is key for any leader in a new role is to consider the areas in which they need to give a particular lead and where they deliberately support and follow the lead given by others.

An important question to reflect on when anyone is in a new role is why should anyone follow their lead? How best do they build credibility and be convincing in the way they describe desired outcomes? How can they communicate in a way that encourages and builds commitment and motivation, so that they inspire the ambivalent?

As you approach a new role or a new phase, it is worth asking where you need to take engagement deeper and where you need to become more detached in order to give other people the space to take the lead. Practical ways of being constructively disengaged can involve ensuring that there is a clear understanding of what success looks like, recognizing the emotional triggers that can make you overanxious and looking ahead at the risks and being as objective as possible about them.

There is a careful balancing act of being engaged and detached at the same time. Your intuitive judgement may well be weighing up different factors which enables you to adjust your approach. It can be helpful to think through what the risks are if you become more detached, and whether, if you become more engaged, this would be welcomed or resisted.

Balancing principle and pragmatism is never straightforward but it is always worth addressing carefully. There will be circumstances where it has been helpful to focus strongly on principles rather than pragmatism. There might have been occasions where being purely pragmatic has led to others questioning your values and feeling that you have let them down. Careful explanation is then needed about why you took the actions you did.

There is a balance between awareness and action. Being a good listener enables you to observe the undercurrents and risks. Keeping a virtuous circle of awareness and action enables us to learn from experience, recognizing the risk of continuing to put off a decision. What often helps is being deliberate in standing back and observing, and then testing out choices with others before finalizing them.

Fundamental to making choices is how we weigh up data from our emotions and our rational brain. Our emotional antennae might kick in quite quickly and result in reactions of 'fight or flight'. Our rational brain may take longer to distil what we are hearing, hence the importance of sitting outside ourselves and observing our emotions and seeking to separate reactions, useful insights and background noise.

Not all our choices will make us popular. When I resisted taking on an additional area of work on schools' policy, I was chastised, rightly, by my boss for the manner in which I had expressed my concern. In the area of nursery education, I was resistant to taking on more staff: it was the then Finance Director, Leigh Lewis, who was insistent that I needed additional resources. I am forever grateful to Leigh for bringing a sense of realism to my 'hair shirt' mindset.

After high-profile problems with the examinations system in England in 2002, I saw a golden opportunity for a reform in the examination arrangements for those aged 18. I built a strong working relationship with the then Minister of State, working jointly on radically different new certification arrangements. The Minister of State was a strong advocate of this reform, but I had failed to anticipate the scepticism with which the proposals would be viewed by the Secretary of State. I had made a wrong choice about the development and advocacy of a particular set of reforms, thinking I had clear ministerial backing. There was a big lesson here for me about being clearer about the eventual decision makers and building the right alliances with the final arbiters.

At the point of moving on from working in government, I had the offer of a secondment to a coaching organization or work with a national consultancy on education issues. The latter was, in many ways, a more secure route but did not catch my imagination as much. My heart was telling me to pursue the coaching secondment. My head was veering towards the consultancy route. This was a moment to follow my heart, recognizing that coaching could potentially be far more fulfilling than consultancy. I am eternally grateful that I followed my heart and not my head. In following my heart, I used my head to seek to make the right choices in taking forward a second career in coaching. Giving yourself time to reflect on what your head is telling you and what your heart is telling you is key; allow yourself to sleep on decisions or go for a walk before reaching a final conclusion.

Reflections

1. How best do you balance leading and following?
2. How do you want to balance principle and pragmatism going forward?
3. What will help you make choices about the shadow you want to cast in different contexts?

20 Come out of the shadows

Many coaching conversations start from considering what is holding someone back from being the leader they could be. I might ask, what might happen if you look at your experience and opportunities in a different way? How might you be liberated from your inhibitions so that you can be more confident and adventurous?

My colleague Hilary Douglas and I were very conscious that a lot of the people we worked with, especially the women, are held back from seeking leadership responsibilities or do not find it easy to exercise their full leadership influence and authority. When we wrote the book *The Reluctant Leader*, we gave it the subtitle, 'Coming out of the shadows'. The book crystallized what we had sought to do in coaching conversations, encouraging reluctant leaders to take the plunge and bring a greater degree of assertiveness. We encouraged them to view their gifts more dispassionately, be willing to step into the unknown, confront their fear of failure and have the courage of their convictions. We wanted to help them understand how their brain worked, to know their sources of support and to keep a sense of perspective.

The heart of our book was a desire to prompt leaders to come out of the shadows and recognize their sources of authority. For many leaders, what has been key to coming out of the shadows has been believing they can prioritize, using the power of reflection and being more willing to make decisions. At a pragmatic level, it has involved developing ways of engaging effectively with difficult people, accepting that you will not always be popular, and that others will not necessarily think like they do.

Practical messages for those seeking to come out of the shadows include believing in their right to be at the top table, knowing what keeps them fresh and energized, not being over-shadowed by their predecessors and the reputations of previous leaders. We saw coming out of the shadows as a natural progression as an individual moves into a more senior role when someone retires. Sometimes a more exposed role can be thrust upon us when someone unexpectedly moves on, or events result in a high profile for a previously relatively neglected area.

Unexpected events can increase the spotlight on us, especially if we have not anticipated the way our comments or decisions will be interpreted. Our inclination may be to retreat into the shadows when what is needed is an acceptance of the context we find ourselves in, alongside the need to speak as calmly as possible to clarify what has happened and seek a measured way forward.

Moments when I have come out of the shadows were either where the person I was working for moved on, or there was an impending crisis that had to be resolved. When Jim Hamilton was appointed head of the Education Department in succession to Bill Pile, I was the key bridge between the department and its new head at the age of 26. After Mark Carlisle was replaced as Secretary of State of the Education Department by Keith Joseph, I was the initial interpreter between an ambitious and radical Secretary of State and a cautious department.

When I inherited the leadership of the grant-maintained Schools Division, there was a major impending issue about financial calculations which had to be addressed pragmatically and quickly where I needed to put a clear recommendation to Ministers that would not be popular. Thankfully the then Secretary of State Kenneth Clarke readily accepted a pragmatic solution which stood the test of time over the next decade.

There were a couple of similar occasions when, as the Finance Director General, I had to be unequivocal about the risks that needed to be avoided. I built open communication and a high level of mutual trust with both the Treasury and the National Audit Office. These relationships were extremely valuable when there was a risk of misunderstanding or suspicion.

I am conscious that at different points of my working life, and in leadership roles outside work, I have not been decisive enough on some performance issues. I have tended to give people the benefit of the doubt and believed that they would learn from experience and make the improvements in their focus and performance that were needed. I always wanted to be charitable and encouraging, but stayed in the shadows too much sometimes when decisive action was needed.

I will often say in my coaching work that I draw from my failures more than my successes. I quite often invite people I work with to reflect on whether they are staying in the shadows too much or whether they might be more explicit in their voice and the use of their authority.

I admire the judges I have worked with in the UK, Australia and Bermuda. They have to explicitly weigh up the evidence presented to them and make judgements or give clear advice to jurors. When they express a judgement, they know that it will be fully in the public domain and can be appealed. They have learnt the skill of using words in a way that brings clarity to the law. They unashamedly do not hide in the shadows.

When I work with individual leaders, I encourage them to reflect on what the appropriate balance is between when they are rightly in the shadows and when they need to be explicit and clear in unashamedly expressing their views. There are times to be in the shadows and let others be in the limelight. There are occasions when hiding in the shadows is an abdication of responsibility.

Reflections

1. When might you have stayed in the shadows for too long?
2. What might release you from your inhibitions and enable you to move out of the shadows?
3. How will you balance being in the shadows and the limelight going forward?

E

Live With Your Emotions

Our emotions give us very valuable data about what is going on in particular situations. Our emotional antennae are often working faster than our rational brain, but our emotions can also exaggerate the risks and make us more wary than we need to be. What is key is to recognize when an emotional reaction is beginning and use that as data before we are captured by an emotional reaction that can distort and undermine us.

This section deals with five emotions that can derail us. Perhaps we have to accept the inevitability that from time to time they will throw us off course and be difficult to deal with. These are emotions we cannot ignore and just brazen our way through. To move on we need a narrative that allows us to accept what has happened and not let past emotions exhaust us or the way we want to move forward.

There are many other emotions that can derail us, such as fear, pride, shame or anger. In this chapter, I will cover five emotions that I have had to learn to deal with and am often addressing in coaching conversations.

21 Unfairness

Unfairness is a fact of life. (Admittedly, unfairness is not an emotion, although given that we can acutely feel the unfairness of things, it is a useful shorthand for all the emotions that can arise as a result of injustice.) Justice and fairness for one person will be interpreted as unfairness for someone else. The tendency to appoint men to senior roles in the twentieth century was grossly unfair to women. In the eyes of some, the appointment of many more women into senior positions in recent years has felt discriminatory to some men. But men had enjoyed privileges for far longer than they deserved. The fact that some people excel in interviews has given them an advantage when competing with other interviewees who are not at their best in that context, even when organizations seek to take a range of factors into account in their recruitment processes.

Looking back, there may be occasions when you have benefitted from a prior relationship when it has come to an appointment. On other occasions, you may have felt it very unfair that the choice has gone to someone else, and resented it. Social and legal expectations about merit, fairness and inclusion have thankfully progressed over recent decades, yet human and organizational fallibility remains in various insidious forms.

It can be helpful to reflect on what the balance has been between when decisions have gone your way or in favour of others and to be philosophic about the inevitability of this happening. We seek to build fairness into the decisions we make but there are inevitably biases that will affect our judgement, however hard we try to observe the risk of bias and counter its effects.

Looking ahead, we want to be treated with a reasonable degree of fairness but need to be pragmatic in that our lens on fairness may be very different to others'. Appointments are rarely made purely on individual merit. In any team there needs to be the right mix of skills which will mean that the credentials of different people will need to be weighed up according to the perspectives of those doing the appointment. If we play the fairness card too hard, we may end up feeling self-righteous and potentially resentful.

There are a number of occasions in my career in government when I was selected for a role where other people might have felt it was unfair. I was appointed Principal Private Secretary to Mark Carlisle, the Secretary of State for Education and Science, in 1979 over a more experienced candidate partially because I had had some dealings with Mark Carlisle on potential legislation when he was the Opposition Education spokesman:

hence there was already a degree of trust. I was appointed Press Secretary to Kenneth Baker, a subsequent Secretary of State for Education and Science, having worked closely with him on a piece of controversial legislation. I was appointed the Director General for Finance in the Education and Employment Department, having built a strong working relationship with David Blunkett, the then Secretary of State.

On the other hand, I ceased to be Press Secretary after Kenneth Baker moved on because his successor wanted to bring his own press secretary from his previous role. A reorganization of the senior leadership at the Education and Skills Department to bring in a university vice chancellor meant that my post ceased to exist. There were moments when I initially felt unfairly treated and had to 'get over myself'. On both occasions, the eventual outcome was fine. It just took some time for me to hold my nerve in these two situations before next steps opened up. The consequence of leaving the Director General post was the prompt to move into coaching as a second career, which was one of the best decisions I ever made, even though it was prompted by unwelcome and uncomfortable circumstances.

In my coaching conversations I sometimes ask individuals if they feel as if they had been treated unfairly. This question has often been a trigger revealing deep emotion. Once people have articulated this sense of unfairness and got it 'out of their system', they become more reconciled to what has happened and are able to move on. For some, the sense of unfairness can take a tight hold and be very constricting. I invite people to reflect on when decisions that have benefited them might have felt unfair to others. I invite them to reflect on what the overall balance is between the times they have been the beneficiary of apparent unfairness and when they feel they have lost out.

Reflections

1. When have you felt gripped by unfairness and what enabled you to move on?
2. What has been the balance for you, in terms of fairness, of when decisions have appeared to favour you or been to your disadvantage?
3. How best do you demonstrate fairness when making decisions and articulate your reasons so that others feel that their case has been properly considered?

22 Rejection

Rejection is a very different emotion to unfairness. You may feel that a decision about an appointment was fair with another candidate being better qualified, yet you perfectly understandably feel a sense of rejection. This can be particular acute when you have been considered for a sequence of roles and have not been selected for any of them. Rejection can lead to a refinement in your narrative and approach, which increases the prospect of success in due course. Rejection can also be helpful in prompting a review about whether a change of direction or priority would now be appropriate.

Where the emotional reaction of rejection can be more difficult to overcome is if it reinforces a sense of rejection from your formative years. A fear of rejection can lead to blanking out potentially unwelcome messages from colleagues and not wanting to hear feedback that could reinforce this sense of rejection. As you explore new avenues, there is bound to be a degree of rejection. Others may well not see you as matching their particular needs. Their rejection is often helpful and avoids the risk of your taking on responsibilities to which you are not fully suited.

When you feel rejected, it is always worth seeking to stand back and understand the reasons why you have not been successful on this occasion. The perspective of a third party can be invaluable as they can observe and comment in a way which is not distorted by an emotional reaction.

In 1975, I was fully immersed in the board-level role of Director of Services for the Department for Education which included leading on HR, IT and Analytic Services. The Prime Minister (John Major) decided to merge the Education and Employment Departments with immediate effect. I worked closely with my opposite number at the Department of Employment (David Normington) to begin the work on merging the two departments. It was a slightly rude awakening when someone said to me, 'You do realize there will only be one Head of HR and Services in the new Department.'

There was a very full and fair process to make appointments to the new Executive Board with David being successful in taking on the board-level post. After a couple of hours of feeling an intense sense of rejection, I accepted the outcome. I offered to put together a plan on communications for the combined Department and was asked to lead a senior management review to decide on the structure of the new Department. I was back on the board of the combined Department as the Finance Director within 18 months.

I had worked closely with a number of secretaries of state over a 30-year period but had much less rapport with Charles Clarke, partially because I had committed myself to supporting a set of policies being developed by the Minister of State (David Miliband) which were then not taken forward by the Secretary of State. I had to recognize that he wanted a person with a very different background as a Director General, and it was therefore time to move on.

It is good practice in coaching to have chemistry meetings between the coach and potential coachee. It is normally clear during a chemistry meeting if a coaching relationship is going to be productive and enjoyable for both people. Sometimes you think a coaching relationship would work well but the individual decides not to work with you. Sometimes you can feel rejected when you are turned down, on other occasions you feel a sense of relief. I always say to people that if they have any doubts about working with me, they should decide to work with someone else. If anyone starts a coaching relationship out of a sense of obligation it is unlikely to be fully open and engaging.

I quite often talk with people in coaching conversations about the sense of rejection and when it is helpful to name that sensation early and work it through with a colleague or coach.

Reflections

1. When has a rejection been helpful in saving you from a context which would not have been fully satisfying?
2. When have you felt a sense of rejection and still pursued the same course of action and then regretted your persistence?
3. When has there been a sense of relief when you have been rejected and have thereby felt liberated to move on?

23 Grief

Grief can affect us at both a personal and professional level. Grief in our families can have an effect on us for at least a couple of years. We may throw ourselves into our work, but there will be a sadness that can be all-pervading and take away the joy from our work.

Professional grief can take many different forms. There is the grief when a patient dies, a pupil continually misbehaves, a prison inmate becomes violent, a project is cancelled, a product fails, a staff unit is abolished or redundancies are declared. Grief can hit when considerable effort and focus has gone into a particular person or approach which is terminated or rejected. We are expected just to move on and deal with the next patient, pupil, project or task, but grief doesn't go away that easily. Grief has to be worked through so that disbelief can move into anger and can be allowed over time to become acceptance.

When we move on from one role to the next there will be times of grief. We may have worked hard to build a team or to take a project to its next level. When students or pupils move on, there is a satisfaction in the progress they have made along-side an element of grief that relationships that have been built up will not be continuing in the same format. The sense of grief may be accentuated when some people move on happily with no regrets, whereas a degree of grief is felt more acutely by you than by others.

As people think about moving on to different roles, I encourage them to think through the element of excitement about change on the one hand, and grief about changes on the other. It is often better to anticipate a degree of grief and prepare for it rather than pretend it won't exist. I sometimes suggest to people that they be deliberate in spending a short period of time expressing and sharing their grief: releasing that grief can then help them move on with less anguish.

When the work of a team is going to come to an end, I encourage people to think about what they have succeeded in doing as a team, what other happy memories they have of working as a team and what they will miss about the shared endeavour. Having talked about what they will miss, there can be an element of shared grief which helps all the participants move on with a greater degree of acceptance about the inevitability of change.

I enjoyed working very closely with Mark Carlisle in his role as Secretary of State for Education and Science at the start of Margaret Thatcher's term of office in 1979. We knew that his tenure as Secretary of State could be limited as he was not as politically aligned with the Prime Minister as some of his colleagues. It was not a total surprise when he was stood down from the Cabinet in 1991.

Mark wanted to have a farewell party in his office. We knew that Sir Keith Joseph would be his successor and was going to arrive at the office at 7.00p.m. with the required reading list for his senior officials. A farewell party for Mark Carlisle was still in full swing at 6.00p.m. We had to usher Mark out of the building and then clear the office as fast as we could so there was a sense of calmness ready for the arrival of his successor. Because the change of Secretary of State took place so quickly, there was no time to grieve, especially as Keith Joseph had an agenda that he perfectly reasonably expected us to be implementing straightaway.

When the Department for Education was merged with the Department for Employment in 1995, I organized a wake for 200 senior people from the Education Department. What helped colleagues accept the rapid change was that there was a strong justification for the merger, as it would bring the political lead and funding for further education and technical education within one Department rather than being split between two Departments. Even so, there was considerable unease and apprehension.

I gave a speech at this party thanking people for their significant contributions. I based my speech around the passage from Ecclesiastes which incorporates the following lines:

There is a time for everything,
And a season for everything under the heavens:
A time to be born and a time to die
A time to plant and a time to uproot
A time to tear down and a time to build
A time to weep and a time to laugh
A time to mourn and a time to dance
A time to scatter stones and a time to gather them
A time to keep and a time to throw away
A time to tear and a time to mend.
(Ecclesiastes 3.1–7a, NIV)

The event was a cathartic release of emotion and proved very therapeutic. It enabled people to move into a different frame of mind and begin to see the pluses about the merging of the two Departments. When I have met people over 25 years on from that event, I receive comments about how important that wake had been in enabling people to move into a positive frame of mind about making a success of the combined Department.

I joined The Change Partnership, an executive coaching organization, initially on secondment in 2003 and then permanently in 2004. When I left the Department on secondment there was no sense of grief as I was ready to move on. The grief had been six months earlier when I recognized that it was time to move on.

When a number of us as coaches within The Change Partnership decided to set up our own business called Praesta Partners in 2005, there was an element of grief about leaving the parent business of Whitehead Mann, but this was overlaid by the attractiveness of setting up our own business away from the constraints of an executive search organization.

Since 2005, Praesta Partners has kept evolving with different people coming and going and different governance structures. There has been an inevitable degree of grief as good colleagues have moved on: this has been counterbalanced by the economic reality that we had to keep reinventing the business in the light of a changing market and the evolving preferences of individuals.

Reflections

1. When has grief got in the way of accepting reality?
2. How best have you handled a sense of grief when the work of teams has come to an end or changes have been forced on an organization?
3. How best will you handle future occasions when grief might affect you as you move on in your work life?

24 Disappointment

Disappointment can be an individual emotion or one that is shared by a whole team. The parallels from sport are helpful in illustrating how best to handle disappointment. In any match between two teams, one of them will be disappointed by the result. In a race, everybody other than the first three might be disappointed by the outcome. The disappointment in the sports team might be tempered by a result that was not as big a defeat as they had feared. A runner who is sixth might be absolutely delighted when they exceed their personal best.

When I began doing a Masters' degree in traffic engineering and planning at Bradford University, I was disappointed that I was not enjoying the course as much as I had hoped: that disappointment enabled me to explore other possibilities and led to the conversation that prompted me to apply to the Civil Service.

When I was working in the Treasury and was approached about becoming a Director, I was disappointed that the Permanent Secretary at the Education Department at the time blocked that opening because he wanted to advocate for a more established Director. In 2001, I was disappointed not to have been appointed as the Director General for Public Finance in the Treasury when I was the recommended candidate, but the Chancellor of the Exchequer chose someone else, who had worked with him over a long period.

I had understood from comments made to me by the then Head of the Civil Service in 2002 that I was in the next three to be appointed to Permanent Secretary, but a few months later I had dropped down the priority list. I was the same person making the same type of contribution but needs and circumstances had moved on.

Each of these disappointments felt acute at the time. For each of them it helped that I understood the reasoning that had led to the outcome. What helped in handling disappointment was having continually interesting work, a very supportive family context and a philosophy about life whereby work was only part of life and not what mattered most in life. Having good friends with whom I could talk honestly about my reactions was enormously helpful in enabling me to reframe disappointment into a more positive view about future possibilities.

The experience of different disappointments has been so helpful in my coaching as it has helped me understand where individuals are coming from and how disappointments can affect individuals and teams. When a team becomes disappointed in itself it loses energy and incisiveness. Transmitting a sense of disappointment soon means the energy in a team is eroded. The team can rapidly disappear into self-reflection and get stuck.

It is helpful to reflect on when disappointment is caused by external factors and when the disappointment is about one's own reaction and contribution. In my first career, I was disappointed in myself when I didn't act quickly enough in response to limited performance by some of the individuals I was working with. Sometimes giving people the benefit of the doubt meant I was disappointed in their eventual contribution and performance, but more acutely I was disappointed in myself for not having recognized the root issues early enough.

There were a couple of periods in my first career when I was so preoccupied by what I was going to do in the next role that I became disappointed with my contribution in the current role. Sensing that disappointment in myself was an important signal about where I needed to refocus my energy and address the present reality and not be over concerned about future steps.

As a coach I have often been delighted by the progress that people have made and the outstanding successes that they have delivered. I have also experienced disappointment when individuals have not taken full advantage of the coaching sessions. Sometimes there has been a disappointment in myself that I have not enabled them to progress in the way I and they had hoped.

How we handle disappointment going forward is important as there will be disappointment, just as night follows day. Disappointment will sometimes gnaw away at us, even if we think we are being brave. Perhaps the average week might include four disappointments: if we only count two disappointments at the end of a week, it has been a good week. Perhaps having this sort of measure enables us to be balanced in the way we recognize the inevitability of some degree of disappointment.

Reflections

1. What disappointments have struck you down most acutely?
2. What disappointments have now turned into a relief that a particular opening did not happen?
3. How best might you handle disappointments going forward?

25 Dejection

Dejection can be physical, mental, emotional or spiritual. Dejection is a flatness where we feel exhausted or run down. It might be associated with frustration and be the long-term consequence of relentless working hours and exposure.

Continuous working arrangements that lack variety and are inconducive to well-being can mean slipping into a sense of dejection that dampens the spirits and squashes the soul. When captured by dejection you can feel locked in chains, unable to appreciate the sunlight and wanting to hide away or disappear into oblivion.

Colleagues may be sympathetic if someone is suffering from an obvious physical injury, but there may be little sympathy for damage sustained over a long period that is invisible. We seek to hide our mental frustrations as we may feel humiliated talking of mental anguish or lack of sleep. Being stoic in our demeanour risks making the situation more acute.

Dejection can be all-consuming and create days or weeks of darkness that take a long time to disperse. Periods of depression can be hugely debilitating and sap the energy of those who appear to be physically the most resistant.

As you think about shaping your future, it is worth reflecting on what situations can cause dejection and how best you prepare for, or avoid, those situations. A lot depends on how much choice is available to you. It is worth identifying and weighing up the risks of any future role knocking you emotionally and then having an eye to how best you mitigate the risks.

On the other hand, avoiding situations where there is a risk of dejection can lead to a very dull set of outcomes, which has its own risks. For most of us there needs to be enough challenge to keep us alert and fully engaged, while seeking to ensure the risk of excessive, undermining pressure is minimized or can be anticipated before it happens.

When I returned to the Education Department in 1993 after having spent two years as the Government Regional Director in the Northeast of England, I was both Head of HR and led a major review of the organization of the Department. I was in

effect doing two jobs, both of which I was thoroughly enjoying, but the amount of effort I was putting in took a toll on
my physical well-being. I caught pneumonia and went back to
work too quickly. The result was a period of a few years where
I suffered from chronic fatigue syndrome. I managed to hide
the effect of the chronic fatigue. As I had my own office at
work, I could lie horizontal for half an hour at lunchtime which
rejuvenated me. This experience has been very influential in my
coaching in encouraging people to think about what helps them
preserve their energy in relentless situations.

I had long had an aspiration to become the vice chancellor of
a university. When it was clear that it was right for me to move
on from government in 2003, I applied for a number of different
vice chancellor roles and was on the short list for appointment
at two universities. Such a role would have brought a fulfilment
that would have been an absolute delight. Both roles, however,
would have involved a geographic move which would not have
been welcomed by the family. In retrospect I think my putting a
job possibility above what would have been best for the family
was a mistake in judgement.

At the time I was dejected about not being appointed as a
vice chancellor. As I look back, I am now so relieved that those
opportunities did not materialize. As a coach I have worked
with leadership teams in four universities, individuals in over
ten universities and become a Visiting Professor at eight higher
education establishments. I was seeking to knock on one particular door of entry into higher education, but what opened up
was the opportunity to be influential in universities in a wider
range of roles.

There was a period of three or four years when I used to
wake up at 4.00a.m. most weekday mornings. After a while
the broken sleep pattern felt debilitating and relentless. I did
not find a ready-made solution at that time. Thankfully, for the
last 20 years sleep has not been a problem and I now fall asleep
within five minutes of putting my head on the pillow. It took
a switch of role and taking up long-distance walking that, in
combination, helped make the difference to my sleep patterns.

In many ways dejection is more difficult to deal with than unfairness, rejection, grief or disappointment. Dejection is more emotionally gripping; it can feel almost impossible to move out of its tight grip. For some, a dejection that flows from burn-out can take a very long time to move through. Patience and strong support from colleagues can help gradually alleviate the worst effects. Often radical decisions need to be taken about work and life priorities in order for dejection to be addressed effectively.

Reflections

1. When has dejection had a grip on you and how were you able to handle that?
2. What might be the early warning signs that dejection is about to envelop you?
3. How best do you prepare for the risks of dejection as you make decisions about your own future?

F

Know What Energizes

Our level of energy varies widely depending upon our physical, emotional, mental and spiritual well-being. Our energy levels may go in cycles and will be hugely dependent upon the various pressures on our lives. Knowing what energizes us can unlock how best we spend our time. When I engage with people on themes from the book, *The Four Vs of Leadership: vision, values, value-add and vitality*, it is the topic of vitality that particularly catches people's imagination.

When individuals and teams have a clear purpose that they are strongly committed to, the consequence is often a level of resilience that keeps them going through tough times. Building a sense of shared endeavour with good companions and a wider team is key.

The renewal of body, mind and soul works differently for different people. What is key is being able to withdraw and know how best to seek renewal. Sometimes this is following illness and sadness; sometimes healing comes through engagement and sounds that uplift, which can range from the voices of friends, to music that cheers and uplifts, to waves breaking on the beach. This section explores different ways in which energy might be renewed and sustained.

26 Know which of your purposes are most precious to you

Posing the question, 'What is your purpose in life?' can seem simplistic and banal but the question, 'What are the interconnected purposes that you see as most important in your life?' can ring true.

For most of us, there are an interconnecting set of intents that are important to us. These often include creating a secure home, ensuring a safe environment for the older people in our families and the children closest to us. Intents will include feeding and clothing our family and ensuring that there are precious times with family and friends. Often there are wider purposes that come from our family, culture and faith backgrounds. From our parents we might have inherited the drive to be successful in our chosen areas of work. There may be values from our cultural background that are very important to us in the way we build our future contributions. There may be a strong commitment to community involvement, be it through local charities, sports groups or faith groups.

There is always the risk that one purpose can become dominant, be that related to work, politics, community or religion. How we review the way our different purposes interact and our openness to see these purposes evolve over time is crucial: there are inevitably defining phases when time commitments change radically. This may be when starting a family, when children leave home, when physical or mental health issues become acute, or when there are changes in the work context, particularly when they are forced upon us.

My background in Yorkshire Methodism was rooted in hard work, duty and an obligation to make a difference for good in the community in which one lived. The obligation to 'love your neighbour' was a key tenant of my Methodist upbringing. My mother had a very strong commitment to her family where she was balancing enabling me to grow up alongside a strong commitment to two step-grandchildren from my father's first marriage and to a sister of hers who did not enjoy good mental health.

The family focus has been important for Frances and me, raising three delightful children and thoroughly enjoying our time with them, their spouses and seven grandchildren. We feel so fortunate to have strong family engagement. For a long period, the family were geographically dispersed within the UK. It was a special delight when Ruth and Owen moved to within 400 yards of our home in 2016, and when Colin and Holly, followed by Graham and Anna, moved to within six miles of our home in 2021.

When the family was dispersed, we had a regular pattern of a week-long summer holiday when we all came together. Now that they are closer geographically, it is a joy to have a variety of events together over the year, including theatre trips and park runs (not that all of us participate in the run itself, although all of us enjoy the breakfast afterwards).

It has been a privilege to work as a coach with senior leaders who come with a range of different life purposes. It has been a delight to engage with leaders who describe themselves as Muslim, Hindu, Sikh, Christian, Jewish, Buddhist, Humanist, Atheist or Agnostic. In my coaching work, I seek to bring an understanding rooted in my Christian faith and understanding. A purpose that matters hugely to me is seeking to enable people to find new hope in the toughest of situations.

In the book, *The Mindful Leader: Embodying Christian wisdom*, I seek to draw out how a Christian understanding of resurrection, reconciliation, truth and responsibility can shape the purposes of leaders. In three sections entitled 'Heart', 'Head' and 'Hands', I look at how ideas such as patience, humility, peace, self-control, forgiveness and sacrifice can be embedded in the way we live out our purposes, expressed in how we engage and influence those in our work context, communities and families.

I encourage those I coach to be deliberate about how their faith perspective influences the purposes that are most import-ant to them. My hope in coaching is to create space where people can stand back and link together the purposes that are built into their psyche and those which they have deliberately embraced and shaped. When people take stock at different stages in their lives it gives them a fresh opportunity to recalibrate those purposes and decide where they want to place their energy.

Reflections

1. How have your family and cultural background shaped the purposes that are most precious to you?
2. What are the purposes that flow from your family commitments that matter most to you?
3. What elements of a faith perspective shape your purposes and give you a distinctive resolve?
4. Where are you spending your time and energy, as this illustrates what you are most committed to, and what you are most preoccupied with?

27 Renew your vitality

One afternoon in 2004, I was asked by a senior member of the UK Cabinet Office if I would have individual, half-hour sessions with six participants on a new high potential development scheme the following morning to help them think through their future approach to leadership. On the train from London to Godalming that evening, I decided to use four words as a framework for these conversations, which were vision, values, value-added and vitality. These four Vs resonated with these six leaders, some of whom I keep in regular contact with nearly 20 years later, including Julie Taylor who has written the Foreword to this book.

These four Vs became the underlying framework in my coaching work. They were originally set out in the book *The Four Vs of Leadership*, published by Capstone in 2006 and then updated in the Praesta Insight document, 'The Four Vs of Leadership: an enduring framework', published in 2019.

Applying the four Vs has enabled leaders to become:

- Focused in their personal vision and equipped for greater responsibilities
- Explicit in defining and living their values and in reassessing life priorities against these values
- Clearer about their value-added contributions, drawing out the best in others more effectively, and
- More deliberate in their use of energy, spending quality time on activities that are most important to them, thereby raising and sustaining their vitality.

Key questions that have often been helpful for individuals on the vitality theme have included:

- What is at the heart of what gives you energy and what saps your energy?
- How can you bring an attitude of mind and heart that sustains you in tough times?
- What steps do you now need to take to ration your time so you can use your energy well?
- How do you best renew your freshness and curiosity?

I observe that uncertainty stimulates vitality for some and dampens vitality for others. For some, responsibility has helped focus energy and vitality. For others, apprehensions that flow from responsibility have sapped energy. I often encourage people to ensure that they spend time with those colleagues who help raise their energy rather than sap their energy. I encourage them to reflect on who helps them to be more creative and forward looking. After which conversations do they feel energized and optimistic about the future?

The times when I have felt most vitality in a work context have been in fast-moving situations. I thoroughly enjoyed six years in government private offices, working for two Permanent Secretary Heads of government departments, two Secretaries of State and then Press Secretary and Head of Information for two Secretaries of State. Each day was packed with activity and decisions that needed to be taken immediately. There was a clear focus and little time for distraction.

I recall one occasion when I was so engrossed as Principal Private Secretary to the Cabinet Minister Mark Carlisle that Terry Perks, the Press Secretary, could not get my attention. He flicked his cigarette lighter on and began to set the paper bag alight which contained my lunch: the result was he got my immediate attention.

I am conscious that the adrenalin flowed fast in those six years. Because a lot of the work was here today and gone tomorrow, there wasn't the same ongoing burden of responsibility, and although at the weekends I was tired, I was less preoccupied with work issues than in some later roles.

I was heavily involved in five major pieces of legislation where the focus was relentless. Working for Kenneth Baker on teachers' pay in the 1980s involved taking a Bill through the House of Commons throughout the night, with the House of Commons stages of the Bill completed with 24 hours of continuous sitting. There were moments of exhilaration when vitality kept going far longer than I had expected.

I had the opportunity of leading in a number of areas when major reform was taking place. This included the development of grant-maintained schools, radical changes in teachers' pay and conditions, the introduction of very different local government funding arrangements for education and a huge expansion in nursery education. There were major obstacles to be overcome but there was a political will that helped ensure there were adequate resources and a strong commitment to work together effectively in focused teams.

In all these areas, what proved key was building a strong team of people willing to both work collaboratively and take responsibility for their areas. I saw my role as agreeing with Government Ministers the direction of travel and then equipping my people to focus on how they could move the work forward with focus, energy and a sense of fun if at all possible.

There were moments inevitably when energy levels felt lower. Government Ministers rejected ideas we had worked on, having believed that we had their commitment. The Treasury was implacably opposed to initiatives even though the value for money appeared outstanding. The very different priorities of different Ministers could create stalemate with no thanks being given for work that had been done on a tight timescale that proved nugatory.

There were times when a lot of committed work had been done for government Ministers or Permanent Secretaries who then moved on just at the moment when key decisions were needed. Once the prime sponsor had moved on, the likelihood of buy-in to next steps was much reduced. Sometimes power plays between senior figures meant that the best of ideas were shelved: but often they would come back into vogue a few years later.

These experiences have fed into my understanding when in coaching conversations, especially when I am seeking to enable people to chart a course through difficult contexts where there are conflicting views, but then to be philosophic if the timing is not quite right and even the best of ideas have to be parked for a season.

Reflections

1. In what context is your level of vitality at its best and most readily sustained?
2. What saps your vitality and how best do you reduce the risk of that happening?
3. What enables you to minimize the risk of your vitality dropping significantly after an adverse decision?

28 Build shared endeavour

The old adage, 'a problem shared is a problem halved' has been proved correct again and again. It is not only that two brains are better than one in sorting out a problem. The benefit that flows from a problem being shared can lead to a stronger level of emotional engagement as well as ensuring a problem is looked at through two different lenses. Job-sharing arrangements are often very successful because of the way a mutual commitment builds both loyalty and energy.

The risk of always focusing on shared endeavour is that individual creativity can be stilted, and a sense of personal responsibility can be diluted. There are moments when it is right to recognize that it is my responsibility alone to make a decision or to move forward a particular set of circumstances. On other occasions, it is folly to hold the burden ourselves and not to engage others in a joint enterprise.

In coaching conversations when people are wrestling with an issue, I will encourage them to think through who else has a vested interest and whose participation might be encouraged, and imagination stimulated. The best of leaders have normally built a strong team around them who bring complementary skills. Together they are a much stronger force than they would be individually. They have become 'more than the sum of the parts'.

When I did a coaching programme with Ken Thomson, a Director General in the Scottish Government, we based a whole coaching programme around music metaphors. Ken is an accomplished violinist and chamber orchestra player. We wrote up our thoughts on the parallels between leadership and music in the booklet, *Knowing the Score: what we can learn about leadership from music and musicians*, in which we explored how players in orchestras work most effectively together when they enable each other to be creative. We talked of each player being a voice in the musical dialogue, sometimes leading, sometimes supporting, sometimes challenging or contrasting, sometimes commenting. The relevance for teams included non-verbal communication and responding instinctively to what others are doing.

My strongest experience of building shared endeavour in a work context was after the 1997 General Election. The Department for Education Permanent Secretary, Michael Bichard, had built up a good rapport in advance of the election with David Blunkett who was appointed the Secretary of State for Education and Employment by the incoming Prime Minister, Tony Blair. Five days after the election, there was a team away event over three days involving the new ministerial team and the Executive Board of the Department. This convivial and purposeful gathering of Ministers, officials and special advisors built a strong sense of both purpose and rapport. An excellent quality of human relationships was established which enabled a very strong partnership between Ministers and officials over the early years of the Labour administration.

My working relationship with the Secretary of State was enhanced by joining him on two train journeys to Sheffield and recognizing that the best time to have an informal conversation with him was at 6.30p.m. in his office. When we met as an executive team with David Blunkett, we deliberately tended to sit in the same seats as we had done on previous occasions so that he could anticipate where we were sitting. David Blunkett, being blind, could not see us, but he could tell by our intake of breath when we were wanting to contribute to discussion. This ease of working together enabled the senior team to flourish, working for a Secretary of State who had an energetic, fresh and committed mandate.

When I was seeking to join the coaching organization then called The Change Partnership in 2003, my candidature was viewed with scepticism. I had never worked in a commercial context. I was viewed as someone who had never sold anything in his life so how could he possibly market what he would bring as a coach? My response was that I had been advocating government policy for 30 years and had been reasonably successful. The scepticism continued for a number of months, which I found exasperating, but before long the public sector part of the business, which I was leading, was the fastest growing part of the business.

What then built a sense of collegiality was the decision of most of us at Change Partnership to set up our own business separate from the parent organization. Establishing Praesta Partners brought us together as a group with us all submitting resignation letters on the same day and financially investing in a new enterprise. Over the next few years there were inevitably changes in direction and departures.

In 2017, six of us fundamentally reshaped the business, reducing the overhead costs considerably, and then moved the business into a virtual environment. In 2021, we took another step forward, after four of the six retired, by building a wider partnership with new recruits. Responding to a Covid-19 world, and making virtual coaching arrangements work effectively, provided a strong rationale for building a new sense of shared purpose. Coaches' meetings now always include a business element and a professional development component with a committed desire to be at the forefront of leadership development thinking. What has made a significant difference has been combining the different types of experience that members of the partnership bring.

Over the last four years it has been a delight to teach a module on The Effective Leader as part of an MA programme on Theology, Leadership and Society in Vancouver with Clive Lim. Clive is an entrepreneur from Singapore with an Asian heritage which contrasts with my background as a Caucasian public servant from Europe. We bring different experiences and insights, and have relished our dialogue and learning from each other.

I see an increasing number of teams include members from a variety of cultural and racial backgrounds. Some international management consultancies I work with are exemplars in drawing on the qualities and experiences of people from very different contexts. There has been a breakthrough in recent years in celebrating and drawing on differences effectively rather than seeking to build monochrome teams.

Reflections

1. When has a strong sense of shared endeavour produced outstanding results?
2. Where are the opportunities going forward to build a clear sense of shared endeavour?
3. What can be the most effective remedies when a sense of shared endeavour seems to be eroding?

29 Renew your body, mind and soul

Building resilience is a buzz phrase which everyone agrees with and then usually ignores. When Hilary Douglas and I wrote the booklet, *The Resilient Leader*, we encouraged readers to spot the warning signs of weakening resilience, noticing patterns of behaviours that were eroding energy. We encouraged leaders to identify triggers that could knock them off balance and to know themselves better and be clear what their anchors were. In our work with people on resilience, we encourage them to cultivate a positive mindset and to seek to bring grounded optimism where possible.

At the heart of our approach with individuals and teams in building resilience is encouraging people to protect their wellbeing and create the space and time to think things through. We encourage them to learn from the past and not dwell on what might have been, and to encourage others to be alongside them and validate them. We encourage our coachees to recognize that they always have choices, even if it is just about the attitude they bring to a particular situation.

Renewing body, mind and spirit is greatly helped if there are rhythms in place that use energy deliberately. It might mean building a pattern into your day so that you do the most difficult tasks when you are at your most creative. It might involve knowing who lifts your spirits and who you can have a quick conversation with who will encourage you.

I unashamedly encourage people to be deliberate in looking after their physical, mental, emotional and spiritual well-being. Physical well-being in terms of exercise and fitness; emotional well-being in terms of relationships and friendships; intellectual well-being in terms of wider reading and debate. Spiritual well-being in terms of recognizing their beliefs about life and its purposes and what they sense their vocation or calling is to make a difference in the world.

Long-distance walks have been to me a source of physical, emotional, intellectual and spiritual well-being. I love the sense of movement and progression that comes with long-distance walking. It has been a delight over the last 20 years to do over 40 long-distance walks in the UK, plus the Machu Picchu Trail in Peru and parts of the Camino in Spain. Joys have included the variety of landscapes and appreciation of the changing seasons. The physical movement helps me work through complicated issues.

Often, after a long-distance walk, I can see the way ahead on a particular issue more readily than at the end of a working day. The most enjoyable walks have been in Yorkshire, partially because that is my heritage. There is the delight in conversations with local people, plus the unique landscapes of the Yorkshire Dales, the North Yorkshire Moors and the Yorkshire Wolds. I did my first long-distance walk to mark my 55th birthday, walking across England from Arnside in Cumbria to Saltburn on the Yorkshire coast. I encourage the people I work with to see milestone birthdays as moments to re-evaluate what activities give them new life and a clearer perspective.

For eleven years, a group of us from Godalming did a long-distance walk every year in early May which proved a delightful time of fresh air and companionship exploring different parts of the north of England. Covid-19 restrictions and then ageing limbs have drawn this season to a conclusion, other than a regular Christmas lunch together.

The Executive Board on which I felt most at home was that led by Michael Bichard between 1996 and 2000. When we did periodic away days, I suggested we break up the routine of being sat around a table all day. On a number of occasions, we did a brisk walk part way through the day which became a valuable routine in ensuring the afternoon session was fully engaging. On a couple of other occasions part way through the day, we visited an art gallery with an exposition of a painting providing this break in a busy day.

Recently, my colleague Hilary Douglas and I have been hosting groups of the people we work with at concerts at the Royal Festival Hall. Hearing, for example, Beethoven's Pastoral Symphony after the limitations of Covid-19 over the previous 18 months was a delight for all of us. There was great conversation between people who were working in different contexts with the focus on shared interests and not on work priorities. These concert visits have reinforced for us the importance of building rapport and an understanding that is wider than work issues, as well as the importance of people being refreshed in body, mind and soul.

I have had the privilege of being able to write books about a range of different aspects of leadership, some of which have been written from a theological perspective. The most recent book is called *Those Blessed Leaders* which is about the relevance of the Beatitudes to the way we lead. For me, the Beatitudes are a profound set of truths that transcend different cultures and provide a challenging set of touchstones for any leader whatever their context.

I have deliberately shared this book with people I work with, whether or not they bring a faith perspective, because the Beatitudes contain truths relevant to any leader about clarity, compassion, gentleness, doing the right thing, mercy, purity, peace-making and an acceptance that sometimes as a leader you will feel persecuted. My aim is not to proselytize. It is to share insights that enable people to reach their own conclusions about renewing their body, mind and soul in their context and against a background of their own life story and culture.

Reflections

1. There is a growing acceptance of the idea that walking 10,000 steps a day helps maintain a basic level of health and well-being. How are you doing against that aim? Are there any other forms of exercise that you enjoy and could take up?
2. What is key for you in renewing your body, mind and soul over the forthcoming months?
3. What could derail your equilibrium and how best do you prepare for that possibility?

30 Seek stillness and silence

When going into company offices, I would feel a mild sense of disapproval if I observed a row of people smoking cigarettes adjacent to the front entrance. But I recognized there was some benefit in their stepping outside the building for five minutes, even if it was to smoke. Subsequently I used to encourage people to 'pinch the smokers' trick' and step outside the building for five minutes for a brisk, brief taste of fresh air. Deep breathing of non-filtered air can rebuild alertness which has sagged during a busy few hours.

A senior leader once told me that they began focusing on work on a Sunday evening and then began work early on the Monday morning and were engrossed all day and all evening until late at night. On the Tuesday they were asked about an email they had sent on the Monday: they had no recollection of having sent the email. This was a rude awakening for this busy leader. We talked about the negative consequences of working non-stop, as it could lead to going onto autopilot too regularly and not thinking through things or remembering what had been done.

What came out of that conversation was the notion of 'shafts of stillness'. We talked about creating shafts of stillness which could put a firebreak between busy spells. To some people, this idea of shafts of stillness is an indulgent luxury, but over time, many of the people I engage with have been converted to incorporating shafts of stillness as brief times of re-energizing and revitalizing. A shaft of stillness might be a personal space you move to where you feel uncluttered. It is a moment to breathe, relax and cherish good visual experiences.

Developing the 'mental stillness' muscle can help block out or tolerate external noise. Brief periods can be set aside where you let the unconscious distil what has been going on. As you then come out of a shaft of stillness, you are clearer about your next steps. Sometimes in coaching conversations I will suggest a five-minute break. Even though I may not have been thinking about the coaching conversation in the five minutes, I often find when I re-enter the conversation there is a freshness or a new angle that the brain has been distilling, without my consciously working through issues in a specific way.

Creating shafts of stillness also involves allowing silence in conversations or meetings and not always rushing to fill the space. As a coach I recognize that allowing moments of silence and stillness can be very useful in allowing a conversation to settle so that the key points are distilled in the mind and heart of the person I am working with.

When I moved on from working in government, I spent three days in the Yorkshire Dales before starting work as a coach. I walked up Pen-y-Ghent and Ingleborough and enjoyed the amazing views from these two Yorkshire peaks. There was a stillness looking out over the Yorkshire landscape. That experience helped me move on with equanimity from one phase of life to the next.

The most dramatic time of stillness for Frances and me was when we were on a boat on Doubtful Sound in the New Zealand fjords. The captain turned the engines off and the boat stood still. All we could hear was the sound of the birds. When, on a boat in Glacier Bay in Alaska, the engines were turned off and the boat was stationary, the dominant sound was the periodic carving of the glacier. On both these occasions, 'silence was golden' alongside the distinctive sound of the natural order, be it the birds singing or the glacier carving. More recently, walking in South Georgia and on the Antarctic Peninsula alongside massive colonies of penguins has reinforced the value of spending time observing the sights and sounds of the natural world.

I have always found the rhythms of the sea provide a valuable reminder of the ebbs and flows of life. Sometimes the sea may be still and calm. On other occasions, rough and pounding, but the ebb and flow happens amid the stillness or the storm. For me the tides are a reminder of an equilibrium and a rhythm that has ups and downs. Life ebbs and flows and require us sometimes to stand firm and at other times to go with the flow.

I have found the writings of David Adam about rhythms of life very moving. He was vicar on Holy Isle for many years and wrote meditations in the Celtic tradition. In his book *Tides and Seasons* (SPCK 1989), he writes about ebbs and flows and juxtaposes sentiments like 'joy in giving, joy in receiving'. He talks of 'wisdom in-coming and wisdom out-pouring'. I sought to reflect some of David Adam's approach in my book *Celebrating your Senses* which suggests meditations based on the five senses of hearing, sight, touch, taste and smell. A reflection I wrote on seeing was:

> May I be open to see
> Viewpoints that enlighten me,
> Pictures that shock me,
> Faces that disturb me,
> And hardship that needs to be addressed.
> May I bring
> A sense of responsibility for my future actions,
> Accountability for past actions,
> A determination to tackle difficult problems and
> A lightness which means I do not get bogged down.
> May I use my gift of seeing to
> Build joint understanding with others,
> Create a shared vision for the future,
> Engender a sense of common endeavour, and
> Make sure that progress is forwards
> Rather than backwards.

For all of us there can be special places where we relax and reflect. A pilgrimage to a special place is rarely wasted, although we may be surprised by the nature of our reflections when we allow ourselves to be quiet and open to new sounds and sensations.

Reflections

1. What are moments of stillness or silence that have been most evocative for you?
2. What type of silence can unsettle you and how best do you respond?
3. How can you create context for others to experience stillness and silence?

G

Look Ahead With Grounded Hope

We can often oscillate between optimism and pessimism about the future. We want to see a way forward that is encouraging and even inspiring. On the other hand, we want to be realistic as we are conscious that false hopes can lead to devastation and dejection. Looking ahead with grounded hope is one way of expressing this balance between seeing opportunities while being rooted in realism.

In this section we explore holding lightly to past expectations and being deliberate in seeing future possibilities as well as being open-minded. We look at what it means to build a sustainable future, recognizing that time is precious. We conclude by reflecting on who we particularly want to invest in to enable them to thrive.

31 Hold lightly to past expectations

Expectations are a fact of life. Having clear, agreed expectations can be hugely positive. The problem comes when expectations are unclear, overbearing or never-ending. Living with a variety of expectations is part of daily life. There is a myriad of expectations that we live with drawn from our personal background and our work context. There are patterns of behaviour and norms that we do not want to step beyond.

We place expectations on others and become irritated if they do not meet those expectations. We expect the trains to run on time, the grocery store to stock the goods we want to purchase and the internet connection to be continuous.

There may have been past expectations that have driven us relentlessly on a particular career path. There are expectations on us to be a good teacher or lecturer which means that we are conscientious in preparation and fully engaged in the teaching and interaction with our pupils and students.

There are times when standing back from the expectations upon us can help us begin to feel liberated and open to new possibilities. Sometimes we need to recalibrate the expectations we put on ourselves. We may have been brought up in a particular area of work and have the expectation that we need to complete every specific task on our own. In a managerial role, a reframed expectation might be about enabling others to deliver outcomes rather than being hands-on in delivering the outcomes ourselves.

In coaching conversations, I invite individuals and teams to reflect on the expectations on them and to what extent they are fully appropriate responsibilities or unreasonable burdens. There is a moment when expectations can and should be challenged, allowing a greater priority to be given to the expectations of greatest importance. When expectations are put in rank order there can be a conversation about whether those with the lowest priority can be deleted entirely, as they may be accretions from the past and far less important now.

When working in ministerial private offices, there was a clear expectation that the work of one day was completed that day so there could be a fresh start on the next day. The norm was that in the evening of one day, the necessary instructions and notes of meetings were completed, so there was no hangover to the following day. This expectation taught me how to dictate fast and get the resulting text close to right first time. This skill has been immensely useful as I now send my coachees detailed notes after each session. I also have developed the practice of dictating the first draft of each book during a concentrated 5–8-day period.

When I was in private office, there was an expectation that I would be able to solve every problem. That was flattering but often undeliverable. By force of time passing quickly, the reality was that I was never able to meet everyone's expectations, which helped build a degree of immunity to the disappointment of others.

In some of my leadership roles, there was the legacy from my time in private office of seeking to do too much myself, but I was fortunate enough to have very good people working for me in most of my jobs who rightly restrained me from getting too involved.

I am conscious that people can come into coaching conversations with expectations that are sometimes unrealistic. I seek to help them clarify their own expectations about how they want to shape their careers and work patterns going forward. Part of my role is to help them sit more lightly to the expectations that others place on them. But even more important is helping people recognize the expectations they put on themselves and how those pressures might be eased.

In my early seventies I had expectations about the travelling I wanted to do and the long walks I wanted to complete. The effect of Covid-19 restrictions and a tedious problem with my left foot has put a dampener on those expectations. This has been a reminder about both the value of having some expectations and also sitting lightly to them when circumstances change.

Frances and I had no expectation that our three children and their families would relocate from London and Chester to our local area. They have all done so in the last few years, to our great delight. It was helpful never to have this as an expectation.

I had expected to stay in the Senior Civil Service for the whole of my working life. I am delighted in retrospect that this expectation changed, enabling me to move on into a second career. I share with my coachees my experience of being utterly committed to expectations in one area of work, but then letting those expectations change radically because of changing circumstances well beyond my control.

When my son Graham and I wrote the short book *Living with never-ending expectations*, we suggested that expectations should be tested against the following criteria. Are they relevant to meeting the overall intent of the organization? Do they reasonably take wider circumstances into account? Finally, are they realistic in terms of the availability of time, money and people?

I encourage the people I coach to be hard-nosed in their dialogue with those putting expectations on them. There is a risk that leaders keep expecting more and more with scant regard for the pressures they are putting on their colleagues.

Reflections

1. When have expectations helped shape your future intent and actions?
2. What has forced you to sit lightly to expectations and liberated you to think into future possibilities?
3. What are the current expectations that perhaps need to evolve?

32 See future possibilities and be open-minded

Having moved on from the Civil Service in 2003, I found myself coaching a number of people who were thinking through their own next steps. These conversations helped me crystallize my own thinking in the book *Finding Your Future: the second time around*. It was dedicated to my son Graham who asked me this pertinent question when I was beginning to think about moving on from government work: 'Pretend you are 21 again; what would give you greatest joy going forward?'

In that book I explored different starting points of failure, fear, frustration and fortitude. I encouraged people to take stock of what is important to them in terms of family, friends and fundamentals. Looking forward, the book addressed forgiveness, fascinations, freedom and fasting. It referred to the value of thinking through what foresight, focus, fun and fulfilment might mean for them.

Ten years later, I was struck by the apparent contradiction in the phrase, 'wake up and dream'. That became the title for a book which is dedicated to those I have coached who have woken up to possibilities and taken forward the dreams that are most precious to them. Waking up and dreaming is about combining realism with a sense of adventure. It is an encouragement to daring and imaginative daydreaming. There are situations that provide a wake-up call which prompt us to think about what the opportunities within the new reality are.

Sometimes it is about waking up and feeling the sunshine. What might be the 'alarm clock' that is waking you up? What is the next phase of life we need to wake up and be open to? In terms of how we dream and look forward, I prompt the reader to dream wide awake, anchor their dreams, make space for their dreams, live with broken dreams, be open to move on to different dreams and then turn dreams into plans. Coaching conversations often involve encouraging people to wake up well, dream creatively and create a virtual cycle of sleeping, waking and dreaming.

When people have precise views on future possibilities, I encourage them to be open-minded and to think about the range of possibilities that could be available. I invite them to sit in different possibilities and think through the pros and cons of different options. I invite them to put to one side their initial reservations and dream into different scenarios, exploring the potential joys and frustrations of different types of activity. If they are fixed on one particular full-time activity, I invite them to think into the possibility of a portfolio of different activities or working part-time or in a job-share arrangement.

It is helpful to point to individuals who have made radically different choices in the second half of their working lives. Michael Portillo was a UK Cabinet Minister and a potential leader of the Conservative Party who then left politics and became a hugely successful broadcaster covering both politics and railway travel. Jonathan Sedgwick was Principal Private Secretary to the Home Secretary and a director general in the UK Government. He is now an archdeacon in the Southwark Diocese. A number of people I worked with who were in government are now in senior roles in universities. Other senior government officials I have worked with have moved seamlessly into significant leadership roles in consultancies.

With working lives lasting longer and no official retirement age, there is increased acceptance that people will have different phases in their working lives. Active people in their 60s and 70s taking on leadership roles are ensuring that charities are responsive and play a significant role in communities. Age is increasingly no bar to non-executive leadership roles.

It has been a privilege to work with members of the Senior Judiciary in the UK, Australia and Bermuda. Judges tend not to reach senior roles until their 60s and, therefore, are often moving into senior positions when their friends from university days are retiring. The fact that their leadership blossoms in their 60s results in their often being willing to take on leadership responsibilities well into their 70s.

John Thomas, the former Lord Chief Justice, and Brian Leveson, the former President of the Queen's Bench Division, are exemplars of judges who have kept their vivre and sense of leadership responsibility well into their 70s. Both have been key inspirations for me. I delight in the fact that both of them have contributed forewords to the books I have written. I encourage people to think positively about the next decade of their life and to be open-minded about using their experience and skills in new spheres. I encourage them to be open-minded about possibilities that they had not previously anticipated.

When I moved on from the Government, I had no expectation that I would write books. Soon after I left the department, I was invited to write a short book entitled *Mirroring Jesus as Leader,* in which I explored Jesus' attributes as visionary, servant, teacher, coach, healer and radical. This book became the seed corn for the writing over the subsequent 20 years of 32 books and more than ten booklets. My first career had taught me how to draft quickly and clearly. I had not appreciated that it was a transferable skill until encouraged to write articles and books in my own name.

I invite those I coach to think about what skills are transferable. People who have operated successfully in big organizations can make good chairs, for example, enabling thoughtful conversations to be conducted and clear conclusions drawn from those discussions. People who have had to negotiate with different interests in a work situation are often well equipped to be influential within community activities when negotiation with local authorities or local businesses are key to successful outcomes.

Reflections

1. What are the future possibilities that most catch your imagination?
2. How best can you explore the pros and cons of different possibilities?
3. What might be the skills and interests you bring that could take you into areas or activities that you have not previously considered?

33 Build a sustainable future

In coaching conversations there is a balance between exploring radical future ideas and bringing realism about what is sustainable. Enthusiasm for a particular future has to be tested against whether it is financially viable and what the reaction of significant others in the individual's life would be. A lot of the people I work with have no option other than keeping working. They need to keep fresh in their work and find ways not to become too downhearted.

I was prompted by Una O'Brien when she was the Permanent Secretary at the Department of Health to write a book about keeping up your resolve when work is relentless. The result was the book *Sustaining Leadership: renewing your strength and sparkle*, which sought to enable the reader to:

- Reflect on where they are and what matters most to them
- Reframe their present situation and be open to new possibilities
- Rebalance their ability to stay in control and to embrace the power of simplicity

- Renew their energies by bringing a lighter touch and building a good foundation for the future.

What resonated most with those who worked through the themes in the book were:

- Reflecting on the relevance of past experiences and the new reality they needed to address
- Reframing previous beliefs and attitudes that might be holding them back
- Rebalancing their lives through embracing simplicity
- Decluttering, decomplicating, demystifying and detoxing
- Renewing their approach by resuscitating their heartbeat where the passion for different aspects of life had been lost but remain important.

When Hilary Douglas and I were working extensively with leaders handling challenges following Covid-19, we were conscious that there was an appetite for guidance about creating a sustainable future. Our research told us that leaders who made a sustainable difference and stayed resilient in challenging times united their teams around common goals, whatever the uncertainties of the longer-term. They invited innovative approaches and learnt from disappointment as well as celebrating success. They remained agile to changing circumstances and encouraged collaborative behaviours across barriers and silos.

We found that metaphors often helped catch people's imagination in helping them to see a way forward that could be sustained. In our booklet *Leading for the Long-term: creating a sustainable future*, we explored metaphors that had particularly resonated:

- Seeing the wood for the trees
- Connect with each link in the chain
- Capture the genius of your people
- Stay calm amid the storm
- Float like a butterfly and sting like a bee
- Weave the golden thread of trust.

We have found ourselves coming back to these themes as leaders seek to hold their nerve. We deploy questions like, 'What enables you to be a radiator of energy and not a drain on people's motivation?' and 'What is the shift we each need to make to our mindset and behaviours to enable the whole system to work together effectively?'

Metaphors are a valuable way of catching people's imagination about future possibilities. In the book *The Power of Leadership Metaphors: 200 prompts to create your imagination and creativity*, I delighted in illustrating the relevance of metaphors that were both ancient and current. Ones that particularly resonated with those I coach include, 'the seed has to die for the plant to grow', 'life is not a dress rehearsal', 'the light at the end of the tunnel', 'bottling the positives' and 'looking beyond the end of your nose'. Recognizing the truths in phrases like, 'every tide has its ebb' or 'great oaks from little acorns grow', has helped people build a quiet and determined resolve to look positively into the future. The biggest challenge in writing this book was getting the word count precise so that the book included one metaphor on each page.

Spending a year doing postgraduate studies in Vancouver helped me become open to different types of leadership opportunities. Seeing people move on into different careers after a spell in government helped me become more open-minded about different, future options. I have been fortunate to be in continuous work for 50 years, split between two careers. I recognize that at some point health circumstances will have an overriding effect. I want to keep coaching for as long as people feel I can bring a valuable contribution.

My appointments as a Visiting Professor of Leadership Development at Chester, De Montfort, Surrey and Huddersfield Universities have recently been renewed for three-year periods. There will be a time when I need to reduce my work activities, but I hope that I will be ready to do that with good grace. I have a list of places I want to visit and theatre trips I'd like to do with my grandchildren as the time commitment to working decreases.

Reflections

1. What are the key elements of a sustainable future for you?
2. What will enable you to reframe future possibilities and be renewed and open-minded?
3. What are the most precious elements you want to ensure are part of your future activities?

34 Recognize time is precious

Time is perhaps the biggest gift we have been given. When each day has gone it has passed for ever. When we are enjoying a good book or film, time passes fast. When we are bored, time goes ever so slowly. We can play games with time. I boil eggs for breakfast each morning. I have become increasing adept at using the five minutes when the egg is boiling for different tasks.

There are occasions when having no sense of time is a blessing as we enjoy sitting in the sun or watching grandchildren play. Sometimes time is a curse when so much has to be fitted into limited time and we feel we are rushing from one task to another, doing none of them well.

At different phases of life, we are captive to others' demands on how we use our time, whether that is the demanding boss or the crying baby. But when something is really important for us, we can usually carve out the time to ensure it happens. If Christian, Hindu, Muslim, Sikh, Buddhist or Jewish worship is important to us, we normally can carve out the time to spend in a reflective space. If meditation is critical to our welfare, it is normally possible to create some space for that to happen by contracting with ourselves and others.

I often invite people I work with to reflect on what times are most joyful and fulfilling, and what helps ensure that these enriching times happen. I invite people to reflect on what times are most trying for them and how best they can prepare for such moments and even reframe them in their minds so that there is a purpose or an acceptance of these trying times.

When people are contemplating changes in their work commitments, I invite them to think about the ideal mix of how they want to spend their time set against the reality of the expectations on them going forward. I suggest that they might score out of ten the enjoyment and fulfilment level in different ways of spending their time to help create a plan for the mix of activities that will give them most satisfaction.

As people are living longer, I encourage them to reflect on how they want to use the time left to them across the whole of their lives in a more deliberate way so they can balance personal and work interests with a clear sense of who it is they want to spend time with, and what quality time with different people would look like.

Having embarked on my first career at the age of 23, it felt like there were many years ahead of me. In the early 1970s, people saw careers as for life: much has changed in the last decades with more churn in the nature of jobs and the assumption that people will be willing and able to adapt to a range of different work contexts.

I was conscious that my father died when he was still in full-time work and my half-brother (who was 24 years older than me) had a major debilitating health issue shortly before he was due to retire. I am finishing this book on my 73rd birthday and am not seeking retirement. I love the wider engagement with people and issues and do not want to become 'Grumpy of Godalming'. Whatever time we have available is precious and gives us an opportunity to explore different interests and share experiences. The Founding Principal at Regent College, Jim Houston, was still writing books well into his 90s and had been invited to speak at a conference on his 100th birthday. He was not focused on retirement quite yet.

In my Civil Service career, I was fortunate enough to do 19 roles in 32 years. There was a gift of variety that helped keep me alert and fresh. I opted to do jobs that were full on and worked longer than my contracted hours. The weekends and holidays were very precious, family times.

I do think that contemporary working practices are so much more conducive to family life. The opportunity for virtual working allows for much more involvement of parents in the upbringing of children than is ever possible with a long daily commute. The acceptance of flexible working, part-time working and job-sharing has revolutionized the way families can use time and has reshaped parenthood in a way that was not anticipated 50 years ago.

I was willing to volunteer to do roles that were inevitably going to be time-demanding, such as being in private office and leading on policy areas in difficulty. In doing this I was seeking to live out both aspirations from my background and seeking to bring a Christian understanding into senior decision-making. In the modern era I think I would not have made quite the same decisions. I would have been much more open to job-sharing and to taking longer breaks between roles than was acceptable in the second half of the twentieth century.

Reflections

1. What are your priorities for your use of time over the next few years?
2. How best do you anticipate which use of your time will give you the most joy and satisfaction and then build them into your routines?
3. How best do you ensure that you do not allow the time you have been given to pass by in ways you will, in retrospect, feel have been wasted?

35 Be deliberate in whom you invest

When you shape your future contribution, it is worth reflecting on who might benefit from the contribution you are hoping to make. There are some decisions that directly benefit us rather than other people: this is absolutely fine when our physical and mental well-being needs to take priority. I enjoy long-distance walks because it is on these occasions that I think most clearly. I hope others get some of the benefit from the relaxation that comes from long walks.

I enjoy reading biographies and understanding how people have made choices in their lives: this is partially a personal fascination, but also feeds into the coaching work I do. Travelling and meeting people living in different countries is partially an indulgence, but it also feeds through into the teaching I do with groups of students who come from very different cultural backgrounds. It has been a delight to be investing time in working jointly with Clive Lim with whom I co-teach a module on an MA programme in leadership, theology and society at Regent College on the campus of the University of British Columbia in Vancouver that draws students from across the globe.

It was a delight to write the book, *The Emerging Leader: stepping up in leadership* with Colin, my younger son who was at that stage an emerging leader. Colin had represented Great Britain in international sport and had been thrust into leadership responsibilities in his sporting activities. We distilled our shared understanding of how best leadership qualities are developed in young leaders. We focused on understanding yourself and those you work with, enjoying the journey, knowing your foibles, keeping alert and embedding learning.

We addressed giving steers about how best to move up to a higher level of responsibility through being willing to take responsibility, setting future direction, handling conflict effectively, keeping up communication and making decisions. Our aim was to help equip people to be confident in their developing strengths, sit lightly to uncertainty and develop an understanding of possible, different ways forward. We emphasized the importance of being able to laugh at yourself and recognize when a new direction needs to be taken.

As I look back on my first career, I take huge satisfaction in knowing that many of those who worked for me went on to become senior leaders in different spheres, which included a number of people who became Director Generals and Chief Executives. The greatest delight in coaching is to see the way people's careers progress and their leadership matures. I have coached eight heads of UK Government departments and a further eight individuals on their journey to the Permanent Secretary role. It has been a delight to work in different phases with some people over the best part of two decades, seeking to provide a context where they could articulate and own their developing leadership role. I hope the space I created helped them shape their mindset and approach so that they could sustain the relentless pressures of leadership roles where they were expected to be available 24/7.

Equally satisfying has been working with people as they have moved from full-time employment into a portfolio of activities where they have been able to follow particular interests. It is a reassurance to receive notes from people who describe our conversations as having had a lasting impact on the way they have handled leadership challenges and have found a new balance between personal and work activities.

As a Licensed Lay Minister in the local Anglican church, I have wanted to contribute but inevitably there are time constraints because of working full time. My priority has been to mentor individuals both in the church locally and in the diocese. In the talks I give in the sermon slot, I seek to interrelate insights from the Christian faith to the work context. This is a valuable discipline for me and, hopefully, has a benefit for others. Our congregations include those who find it difficult to hold down a job, alongside those in positions of national leadership. I hope, in some way, I can bring a message of grounded hope to whoever is in the congregation irrespective of their life circumstances.

My steer to all those I engage with as coach, university professor, author or lay minister is to think about who they are investing in and how best they enable others to grow in knowledge, wisdom and understanding. A coaching approach has been invaluable in enabling others to shape their futures.

Reflections

1. Whose development do you take most pride in?
2. Which groups of people would you most like to invest in over the next phase?
3. What do you want to be remembered for by those people in whom you invest?

Concluding Themes

This chapter invites you to reflect on three interrelated themes on shaping your future leadership. These themes cover *alignment*, *acceptance* and *adventure*. It is the interaction between these three themes that brings clarity of intent and an integration between different priorities and emotions.

Alignment flows from recognizing the contributions you can make in your work, the community and your family. It involves having a clear narrative about 'what you are about' and what your purposes in life are. It includes building and articulating clear interconnections between what is meaningful for you and your different interrelated purposes.

What is key is seeking to build a reasonable degree of alignment within yourself, your roles and with the people around you. At the heart of being aligned is seeking to ensure that you are acting in harmony with the people and those endeavours that are important to you, without being captured by particular philosophies or becoming the possession of someone else.

Alignment involves looking for patterns in your behaviours and reactions and those of others, and being mindful of the risk of repeat behaviours. Keeping your equilibrium includes aligning yourself and your aspirations with those who bring out the best in you, especially where there is a shared purpose. Keeping aligned involves being acutely aware of what external or internal factors can derail you and disrupt the alignment you have built within yourself, with your purposes and the people who are important to you.

Acceptance starts from a clear understanding of your own strengths and foibles. It involves recognizing what the best version of yourself is and how that persona is nurtured and encouraged.

What is important is understanding your place in the world, recognizing where things are what they are, and where you can seek to make a difference. It involves understanding your emotional reactions so that you can foresee when your emotions might wrong-foot you, or when there could be a misalignment of emotions that will disrupt your equilibrium or sap your energy.

Acceptance involves not trying to do everything or 'boil the ocean'. Maintaining your equilibrium requires being willing to prioritize and saying 'no' to what would be an unreasonable stretch. It is about keeping capacity available and being mindful when you can become unbalanced. Part of acceptance includes knowing what a state of peace, stillness or grace is for you, and being ready to put yourself in the right context and with the right people to enable a sense of inner equilibrium and joy to be securely there.

Acceptance necessitates being willing to be authentic to yourself in situations you might find different or difficult. It includes having the courage to be yourself, listening carefully to others but then bringing your own unique contribution, mindful of the context that you are speaking into. At the heart of acceptance is a recognition of your unique personality and contribution, alongside an alertness to the potential damaging pressures of group think.

Shaping your future leadership requires a sense of *adventure* and an openness to being bold. It includes the intent to build integration and variety into your life with careful management of time and energy. It involves looking forwards and not backwards and being willing to be adaptive and deliberate in making choices.

At the heart of being adventurous is an openness to trying different things and approaches and not have 'all your eggs in one basket'. It involves being open to what might come together to energize and lift you. It can include being deliberate in the attachments that you seek out with people of different ages, contexts and cultures. It may well mean letting go of some attachments that have been holding you back and restricting your perspectives.

Being adventurous will include recognizing what is precious

to you and ensuring that is preserved, while being open to new ideas and different ventures. Waking up to new dreams and opportunities and being willing to be bold in following them is central, as is not being held back by previous inhibitions or the expectations of others.

Being adventurous includes recognizing the voice and authority you bring in situations when truth is being manipulated and evidence presented in a biased way. It can involve speaking truth when you observe bogus arguments being presented or duplicitous behaviours being exhibited. The effect of social media and the pressure for immediate action can mean poorly-thought-through perspectives and decisions. A test for all leaders is whether they are honest and bold enough to maintain integrity and truthfulness when there is a weight of expectation to conform to the latest set of expectations from those in powerful roles.

Because of changing circumstances in our health, families and finances, there is likely to be a continuous process of realignment of priorities, alongside having to accept different limitations. But there is always the scope to be open to possibilities and a sense of adventure, whatever the changing context might be.

My hope for you is that the prompts in this book will have enabled you to be more aligned with yourself and your inner aspirations and feelings, to be more accepting of the realities you have to address and more focused in your sense of adventure, which will then reinforce the purposes that are important to you and the alignments within yourself, your roles and the people around you.

Reflections

1. What is the most important frame of mind you want to bring to reinforce the alignments within yourself and with your roles and the people around you?
2. What do you need to be more accepting of, so that your sense of equilibrium feels both adaptable and resilient?
3. Where is your sense of adventure going to take you next and how might you be bold in following your dreams?

Acknowledgements

I am very grateful to a number of people who have read earlier versions of the manuscript and offered insightful comments. In particular I want to thank Ruth Sinclair, Ruth Ackroyd, Hilary Douglas, Clare Sumner and Jenny Oldroyd.

I am particularly grateful to Julie Taylor who both gave me valuable comments on the text and has written a thoughtful foreword. I have known Julie for nearly 20 years and have always learnt a huge amount about the response of different leaders through our conversations. Julie is one of the quickest thinkers I have had the privilege of working with: she brings an insightful mind and a deep appreciation of how people are likely to react emotionally under pressure.

I am conscious that my thinking has been shaped by the range of leaders I have worked with. Their willingness to keep learning and adapting has been the hallmark of such impressive leaders as Sunil Patel, Shaun McNally, Charlie Massey and Shaheen Sayed. I am grateful for what I have learnt from the many people I have had the privilege of walking alongside on their leadership journeys.

Tracy Easthope has managed my time with great skill, always bringing calmness and a constructive way of solving problems. Jackie Tookey has provided wonderful typing support, bringing accuracy and consistency in all she does. Both Tracy and Jackie have been cheerful members of the team, without whose support I would not still be working.

I am grateful to Christine Smith who commissioned the manuscript and has been an outstanding editor at Canterbury Press over a number of years. Rachel Geddes has been meticulous in her thoughtful editing of the text for publication.

I am grateful to my elder son, Graham, for suggesting that I write a book that is far more autobiographic than my other books. Our daughter, Ruth, always brings a very practical approach to leadership and communication and is an exemplar of balancing a range of different responsibilities. Our younger son, Colin, always brings insightful observations, having worked with a range of senior leaders in high pressure situations. A particular thanks goes to Frances for her support and encouragement in many different areas of life, and for shaping my thinking through her calm and wise perspectives.

Books and Booklets by Peter Shaw

Mirroring Jesus as Leader, Cambridge: Grove, 2004.

Conversation Matters: How to engage effectively with one another, London: Continuum, 2005.

The Four Vs of Leadership: Vision, values, value-added, and vitality, Chichester: Capstone, 2006.

Finding Your Future: The second time around, London: Darton, Longman and Todd, 2006.

Business Coaching: Achieving practical results through effective engagement, Chichester: Capstone, 2007 (co-authored with Robin Linnecar).

Making Difficult Decisions: How to be decisive and get the business done, Chichester: Capstone, 2008.

Deciding Well: A Christian perspective on making decisions as a leader, Vancouver: Regent College Publishing, 2009.

Raise Your Game: How to succeed at work, Chichester: Capstone, 2009.

Effective Christian Leaders in the Global Workplace, Colorado Springs, CO: Authentic/Paternoster, 2010.

Defining Moments: Navigating through business and organisational life, Basingstoke: Palgrave/Macmillan, 2010.

The Reflective Leader: Standing still to move forward, Norwich: Canterbury Press, 2011 (co-authored with Alan Smith).

Thriving in Your Work: How to be motivated and do well in challenging times, London: Marshall Cavendish, 2011.

Getting the Balance Right: Leading and managing well, London: Marshall Cavendish, 2013.

Leading in Demanding Times, Cambridge: Grove, 2013 (co-authored with Graham Shaw).

The Emerging Leader: Stepping up in leadership, Norwich: Canterbury Press, 2013 (co-authored with Colin Shaw).

100 Great Personal Impact Ideas, London: Marshall Cavendish, 2013.

100 Great Coaching Ideas, London: Marshall Cavendish, 2014.

Celebrating Your Senses, Delhi: ISPCK, 2014.

Sustaining Leadership: Renewing your strength and sparkle, Norwich: Canterbury Press, 2014.

100 Great Team Effectiveness Ideas, London: Marshall Cavendish, 2015.

Wake Up and Dream: Stepping into your future, Norwich: Canterbury Press, 2015.

100 Great Building Success Ideas, London: Marshall Cavendish, 2016.

The Reluctant Leader: Coming out of the shadows, Norwich: Canterbury Press, 2016 (co-authored with Hilary Douglas).

100 Great Leading Well Ideas, London: Marshall Cavendish, 2016.

Living with Never-ending Expectations, Vancouver: Regent College Publishing 2017 (co-authored with Graham Shaw).

100 Great Handling Rapid Change Ideas, London: Marshall Cavendish, 2018.

The Mindful Leader: Embodying Christian principles, Norwich: Canterbury Press, 2018.

100 Great Leading Through Frustration Ideas, London: Marshall Cavendish, 2019.

Leadership to the Limits: Freedom and responsibility, Norwich: Canterbury Press, 2020.

The Power of Leadership Metaphors: 200 prompts to stimulate your imagination and creativity, London: Marshall Cavendish, 2021.

Those Blessed Leaders: The relevance of the Beatitudes to the way we lead, Vancouver: Regent College Publishing, 2022.

Booklets

Riding the Rapids, London: Praesta, 2008 (co-authored with Jane Stephens).

Seizing the Future, London: Praesta, 2010 (co-authored with Robin Hindle-Fisher).

Living Leadership: Finding equilibrium, London: Praesta, 2011.

The Age of Agility, London: Praesta, 2012 (co-authored with Steve Wigzell).

Knowing the Score: What we can learn from music and musicians, London: Praesta, 2016 (co-authored with Ken Thompson).

The Resilient Team, London: Praesta, 2017 (co-authored with Hilary Douglas).

Job-sharing: A model for the future workplace?, London: Praesta, 2018 (co-authored with Hilary Douglas).

The Four Vs of Leadership: Vision, values, value-added and vitality, London: Praesta, 2019.

The Resilient Leader, London: Praesta, 2020 (co-authored with Hilary Douglas).

Leading for the Long Term: Creating a sustainable future, London: Praesta, 2021 (co-authored with Hilary Douglas).

Stepping up: Leading with confidence, London: Praesta, 2022 (co-authored with Hilary Douglas).

Copies of the booklets above can be downloaded from the Praesta website: www.praesta.com.

About the Author

Peter Shaw has coached individuals, senior teams and groups across six continents. He is a Visiting Professor of Leadership Development at Chester, De Montfort, Huddersfield, and Surrey Universities, and is a Professorial Fellow at St John's College, Durham University. He has been a member of the Visiting Professorial Faculty at Regent College, Vancouver since 2008 and is a Visiting Professor at the Judicial College in Melbourne. He has written 32 books on aspects of leadership: some have been translated into seven different languages.

Peter's first career was in the UK Government where he worked in five Government Departments and held three Director General posts. Peter has been a member of governing bodies in higher and further education. He is a Licensed Lay Minister (Reader) in the Anglican Church and plays an active role in the Church of England at parish, diocesan and national levels. He is a Lay Canon of Guildford Cathedral and Chair of Guildford Cathedral Council.

Peter holds a doctorate in Leadership Development from Chester University. He was awarded an honorary doctorate at Durham University for 'outstanding service to public life', and an honorary doctorate by Huddersfield University for his contribution to leadership and management.

In his coaching work Peter enables leaders and teams to use their freedoms as leaders to best effect. Peter draws from his wide experience both as a leader and as a coach of leaders in many different contexts. He seeks to bring insights drawn from his experience of leading and coaching, and bring an understanding underpinned by his Christian faith and understanding. His focus is on enabling individuals and teams to step up in their effectiveness so that they have a clear vision about what they are seeking to do, apply the values that are most important to them, know how to bring a distinctive value-add and recognize their sources of vitality.

Peter has completed over 40 long-distance walks in the UK, with the Yorkshire Dales being his most favoured area for walking. Seven grandchildren help him belie the fact that he was born in the first half of the twentieth century.